10/03

THE GALÁPAGOS ISLANDS

Look for these and other books in the
Lucent Endangered Animals and Habitats Series:

The Amazon Rain Forest
The Bald Eagle
Birds of Prey
The Bear
Coral Reefs
The Elephant
The Giant Panda
The Gorilla
The Manatee
The Oceans
The Orangutan
The Rhinoceros
Seals and Sea Lions
The Shark
The Tiger
The Whale
The Wolf

Other related titles in the Lucent Overview Series:

Acid Rain
Endangered Species
Energy Alternatives
Garbage
The Greenhouse Effect
Hazardous Waste
Ocean Pollution
Oil Spills
Ozone
Pesticides
Population
Rainforests
Recycling
Saving the American Wilderness
Vanishing Wetlands
Zoos

THE GALÁPAGOS ISLANDS

BY JAMES BARTER

Endangered
Animals &
Habitats

LUCENT BOOKS

SAN DIEGO, CALIFORNIA

THOMSON

™

GALE

Detroit • New York • San Diego • San Francisco
Boston • New Haven, Conn. • Waterville, Maine
London • Munich

Library of Congress Cataloging-in-Publication Data

Barter, James, 1946–
    The Galápagos Islands / James Barter.
        p. cm. — (Endangered animals & habitats)
    Includes bibliographical references (p.).
    Summary: Describes the Galápagos Islands with their rich and unique
    flora and fauna, regional divisions, invading species, overfishing, eco-
    logical dangers, and conservation measures.
        ISBN 1-56006-920-1 (hardback : alk. paper)
        1. Natural history—Galápagos Islands—Juvenile literature. 2.
    Endangered ecosystems—Galápagos Islands—Juvenile literature. [1.
    Galápagos Islands. 2. Endangered ecosystems.] I. Title. II. Series.
        QH198.G3 B36 2002
        508.866'5—dc21

    2001004589

Contents

INTRODUCTION   6

CHAPTER ONE   10
A Place Like Nowhere Else

CHAPTER TWO   31
Invasive Species

CHAPTER THREE   46
Fishing Threats

CHAPTER FOUR   61
Ecotourism Threats

CHAPTER FIVE   77
Conservation

NOTES   93
ORGANIZATIONS TO CONTACT   97
SUGGESTIONS FOR FURTHER READING   100
WORKS CONSULTED   103
INDEX   106
PICTURE CREDITS   111
ABOUT THE AUTHOR   112

Introduction

THE GALÁPAGOS ISLANDS, lying six hundred miles off the coast of Ecuador, are among nature's best-known and most-valued ecological treasures. This volcanic archipelago, parched virtually year-round by the hot sun, nonetheless manages to sustain a remarkable collection of plants and animals not found on any of the seven continents. Due to the islands' unique flora and fauna, biologists sometimes refer to the Galápagos as the eighth continent.

Research scientists flock to these islands both to study their widely diverse life-forms and to discover conservation strategies that will guarantee the future for their trove of rare and endangered species. As a living laboratory, the Galápagos are unmatched. The renowned French oceanographer and environmentalist Jacques Cousteau described the Galápagos as "one of the few remaining sanctuaries of wildlife. The exceptional and specific nature of the archipelago's ecosystem . . . is, even today, an incomparable field for scientific investigation in biology, physiology and ecology."[1]

The ecosystem that has nurtured so many spectacular life-forms for hundreds of thousands of years, however, is now tilting out of balance and is threatened. Although the archipelago is now a wildlife sanctuary for the study of all of its plants and animals, some of its species are already extinct and others are endangered. In response, teams of researchers from many nations have converged on the islands to learn what forces have upset nature's balance. These scientists aim to study this unusual habitat to understand how they can reestablish the balance that once allowed so many of the islands' species to flourish.

The research teams have identified human beings as the unmistakable cause of the problems in the Galápagos. Over the past three hundred years careless intrusions by people have set in motion a series of events that have threatened the survival of all of the islands' species. As soon as people landed on the islands, they unwittingly introduced changes detrimental to the native Galápagos wildlife and habitats.

Most destructive to the wildlife has been the animals and plants that people introduced to the islands. Dogs, rats, pigs, goats, and a host of other plants and animals began to rampage across the islands, destroying habitats and eating many native Galápagos species. Foreign plants also took root and began to compete with local vegetation for the precious little rainwater that falls each year. Many Galápagos species, failing to either adapt to the invasive life-forms or

Tourists watch sea lions basking on the sandy shore in the Galápagos Islands. Tourism continues to create problems for the islands' wildlife.

compete against them, became extinct, and others dwindled in number to a mere handful.

Today residents and tourists continue to mistreat the fragile ecosystem of the Galápagos. Local fishermen, recklessly removing more fish than is recommended by the Galápagos National Park Service scientists, have drastically altered the biological balance of the sea. The lure of quick profits has led to the near extermination of marine species by local and foreign fishermen, which in turn puts the entire habitat in jeopardy: As individual species disappear, those that remain suffer as the ecosystem tips out of balance.

The Galápagos Islands are located in the Pacific Ocean, 600 miles from the South American Coast.

Thousands of tourists arriving by cruise ships and airliners leave behind mountains of waste and pollute the fragile habitats of some of the islands' endangered animals. Hikers eager to photograph tortoises and the exotic birds inadvertently trample the very vegetation needed by these animals for food and nesting sites.

The future of the Galápagos is uncertain. Although many conservation groups and scientists are hard at work trying to preserve the indigenous flora and fauna, the money to be made from tourism and fishing may undermine the work of conservationists. Jonathan Barry, executive director of the Charles Darwin Foundation, which promotes conservation of the Galápagos, warns, "The Galápagos are headed for disaster. If the twin problems of exotic [foreign] plants and animals and burgeoning human immigration are not dealt with immediately, they will devastate Galápagos."[2]

1

A Place Like Nowhere Else

THE GALÁPAGOS ISLANDS are home to one of the earth's most unusual collections of plants and animals. Nowhere else but on these fifteen major islands and more than one hundred islets can visitors see as vast an array of endemic species—that is, species confined to a single location. The Galápagos collection of endemic species includes rare five-hundred-pound Galápagos tortoises; prehistoric-looking iguanas that sneeze salt from their nostrils; dozens of exotic birds, including the blue-footed boobies; and dozens of plants, such as miconia and scalesia.

The Galápagos are also home to some of nature's most fascinating anomalies. For example, nowhere else can one find penguins, which are usually associated with the freezing temperatures of Antarctica, living side by side in a temperate climate with large land iguanas and flamingos, which typically live in hot tropical climates. This is also the only region in the world where flightless cormorants dive for food in the same waters as marine iguanas specially adapted to forage underwater—the only species of lizard on Earth capable of doing so.

Through more than a million years of evolution, the endemic species of these islands achieved a natural balance that provided enough food and habitat to allow the survival of all species. Thanks to this remarkably balanced ecosystem, today biologists estimate that the islands have retained nearly 95 percent of their original biodiversity—an extraordinarily high percentage compared, for example, to the Hawaiian Islands, which, despite their legendary lushness, have maintained just 55 percent of their native animals.

Galápagos biodiversity

When scientists speak of biodiversity, they are referring to the variety of living organisms in a specific habitat; biodiversity is generally expressed in terms of the numbers of species of plants and animals in that habitat. As part of the process of picturing an ecosystem's biodiversity, scientists attempt to describe and evaluate the composition, abundance, and distribution of local life-forms. A diversity of species is important to the natural functioning of ecosystems and biologists consider the level of biodiversity to be an indication of the health of an ecosystem.

In the Galápagos, biologists estimate the total biodiversity to be more than two thousand species and subspecies.

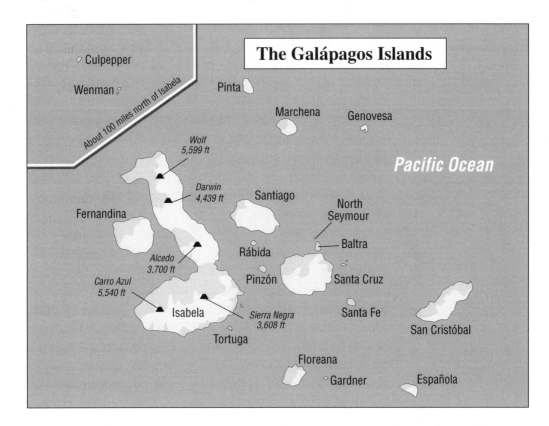

The Galápagos marine iguana is just one of the many animal species that are endemic to the islands.

Biologists consider this an unusually healthy number considering the relatively small landmass of the Galápagos—roughly thirty-three hundred square miles, which is about half the size of the Hawaiian Islands. The biota—the total flora and fauna of the Galápagos—is spread among seven major wildlife groups, and their approximate numbers of species and subspecies are as follows: 1,000 insects, 625 plants, 298 fish, 100 marine invertebrates, 57 birds, 38 reptiles, and 19 mammals.

The biodiversity among endemic species is equally impressive. The number of species found only in the Galápagos is considerably smaller than the total of all species there, yet researchers consider the number quite high compared to comparable islands, such as the Azores, volcanic islands located in the eastern Atlantic. Although the number of endemic insects is not recorded, the number of endemic species and subspecies for the other groups are: 225 plants, 69 fish, 35 reptiles, 26 birds, 30 marine invertebrates, and 4 mammals.

The biodiversity of the Galápagos has long been known. The first person to notice this remarkable quality was the nineteenth-century English naturalist Charles Darwin:

> The natural history of these islands is eminently curious, and well deserves attention. Most of the organic productions are aboriginal [endemic] creations, found nowhere else; there is even a difference between the inhabitants of the different islands. . . . The archipelago is a little world within itself, or rather a satellite attached to America [South America]. . . . Considering the small size of the islands, we feel the more astonished at the number of their aboriginal beings, and at their confined range. Hence, both in space and time, we seem to be brought somewhat near to that great fact—that mystery of mysteries—the first appearance of new beings on this earth.[3]

The exceptionally rich biodiversity first noted by Darwin and later recognized by modern biologists has multiple explanations. Scientists consider the most significant explanation to be the archipelago's variety of habitats. Scientists also cite as particularly important the isolation of the islands far from other landmasses; they also point to the role that chance played in populating the islands in the first place.

English naturalist Charles Darwin visited the islands in the 1830s and was struck by the rich biodiversity he observed.

The plants and animals of the Galápagos thrive in what scientists consider three distinct habitats: island, marine, and coastal. Each of these regions provides a widely varied habitat, enabling a number of different species to live and flourish within their boundaries. Although each region has its unique characteristics and species, each contributes to the well-being of the others, maintaining a healthy ecological balance that has for hundreds of thousands of years ensured the survival of all Galápagos species.

Island region

The island habitat encompasses an unusually rich and exotic variety of mammals, birds, insects, plants, and reptiles.

Charles Darwin

Charles Darwin was born in England on February 12, 1809, to a wealthy family with a long history of interest in science. After Darwin graduated from high school in 1825, he entered the University of Edinburgh to study medicine. In 1827 he quit medical school and entered Cambridge University as a divinity student.

While studying at Cambridge, Darwin found a new interest as an observer of natural phenomena and collecting plants and animals. After graduating from Cambridge in 1831, he learned about a ship named the HMS *Beagle,* which was looking for a naturalist to accompany the crew on a scientific expedition around the world. Darwin joined the expedition.

When Darwin left England aboard the *Beagle,* he had little direction in life and was on the trip with only a mild curiosity about what he would be doing. At the end of the five-year journey around the world, Darwin returned to England with a substantial collection of rocks, plants, animals, and notes and sketches describing all natural phenomena he had observed. For the next twenty years, Darwin studied these notes and sketches and published his findings, which included two important theories. The first was his theory of natural selection, which postulated that each generation of a species will physically improve in response to its habitat over the preceding generations. His second and more profound theory on evolution stated that all related organisms are descended from common ancestors. Moreover, he provided additional evidence that the earth itself is not static but evolving.

Explaining and defending these two theories occupied Darwin for the remainder of his life. The importance of his work was well recognized by his contemporaries yet detested by his enemies, most of whom were clergymen who believed his theories ran counter to the stories of creation told in the Bible. Nonetheless, men of science elected Darwin to the Royal Society and to the French Academy of Sciences. Following his death in 1882, he was further honored by being buried in London's Westminster Abbey beside other great thinkers of England.

Darwin was the first to describe this collection of species and to note that the uniqueness was the result of the warm equatorial location of the Galápagos and the cool waters that flow around the islands: "Considering that these islands are placed directly under the equator, the climate is far from being excessively hot; this seems chiefly caused by the singularly low temperature of the surrounding water, brought here by the great southern Polar current."[4] The unusual combining of the hot and cool climates provided habitats that suited

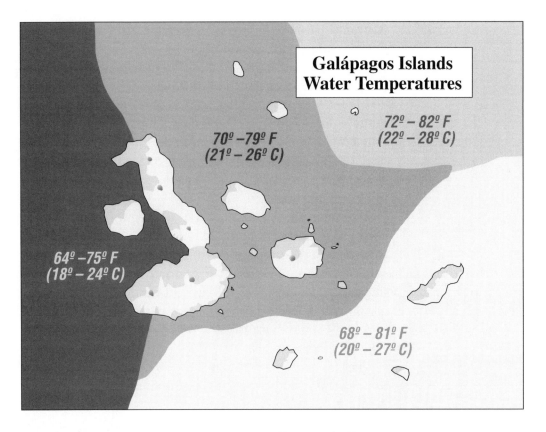

Galápagos Islands Water Temperatures

72º – 82º F
(22º – 28º C)

70º –79º F
(21º – 26º C)

64º –75º F
(18º – 24º C)

68º – 81º F
(20º – 27º C)

the needs of warm-climate species as well as cool-climate species—both in the same place.

The presence of the Galápagos Islands, scattered along the equator six hundred miles off the coast of Ecuador, is the result of 90 million years of volcanic activity. Vulcanologists have identified many extinct volcanoes in the Galápagos archipelago as well as five that have erupted within the past few thousand years and are still considered active. Magma lies ninety miles below the earth's surface, and as the volcanoes erupted, they continued to add mass to the islands. The volcanoes have not only created the islands, but they have also created a sweep of elevations ranging from sea level to fifty-five hundred feet above sea level, which accounts for much of the habitat diversity.

The varying elevations provide suitable habitats to different species of plants and animals. At the higher altitudes, temperatures tend to be lower and the air moister as fog hugs the mountaintops. Conversely, the sea-level habitats tend to be warmer and drier.

Meteorologists explain the different habitats in terms of microclimates that are found throughout the islands. Microclimates are small geographical areas that are close together but experience varying temperatures, rainfall, winds, and humidity. Habitats at sea level, for example, may have one microclimate along the coastline that receives more moisture than a drier microclimate just a few miles inland.

Although the islands lie along the earth's equator, the chilly seas surrounding them generate cooling winds and coastal fog that provides moisture along the coast. As a result of these meteorological characteristics, some island microclimates are hot and support desert wildlife; some are temperate and semiarid with wildlife adapted accordingly; still others are tropical and have wildlife suited to hot, humid conditions.

These island microclimates are responsible for the fact that animals that cannot be found living side by side anywhere else in the world often share the same habitat in the Galápagos. The most well-known example of strange animal combinations is that of the penguin and the flamingo, which everywhere else occupy dramatically different habitats.

Of all of the endemic animals and plants that have thrived on the islands because of the rich variety of habitats, the one that has displayed the greatest diversity is the reptile. This group has managed to exist and evolve into more different species and subspecies than any other animal group. And among these, the one of greatest interest to biologists as well as to conservationists is the Galápagos tortoise.

The Galápagos tortoise

Endemic to the islands, the giant Galápagos tortoise has the highest biodiversity of any species with fourteen different subspecies, eleven of which still survive. Resembling small armored tanks, these primitive-looking animals are the largest tortoises in the world, averaging between three and five hundred pounds. As Darwin noted over 150 years ago, "It required six or eight men to lift them from the ground; and . . . some had afforded as much as two hundred pounds of meat."[5]

Measuring five feet along the arc of the carapace—the back of the shell—these reptiles lumber along at a steady speed of one-eighth of a mile per hour in search of vegetation, which is their only source of food and water. Lacking teeth, the tortoises bite off pieces of cacti, bushes, grasses, or tree branches, and mash them into a pulpy consistency before swallowing. They like to bask in the hot sun during the day and then cool themselves under a shady tree. Occasionally they prefer to wallow in the mud during the wet seasons. The tortoises prefer the hot microclimates and graze on different types of vegetation depending on the microclimate of the different islands.

Darwin observed that some islands produced their own unique subspecies while the larger islands produced two or more subspecies. Each subspecies seems adapted to the local conditions. What Darwin reported, and what modern herpetologists have confirmed, is that each subspecies has a slightly different shaped carapace and neck length.

Divided into fourteen subspecies, the Galapágos tortoise is the most biodiverse species on the islands.

All of the islands' tortoise species fall into two general categories: saddleback and domed. The saddlebacks evolved in dry microclimates void of low-lying grasses and plants, where only scrub bushes, trees, and tall cacti can survive. Forced to forage on vegetation above the ground, the tortoises evolved a U-shaped notch on their carapace near the back of the neck that allows them to stretch their

The Galápagos Tortoise

Although diversity makes each tortoise sub-species unique, the species as a whole has a great deal in common that has sustained its existence. One of the survival techniques, which has enabled the Galápagos tortoise to persevere in the desert environment, is a remarkably slow metabolism. Metabolism is the chemical conversion of food into energy. Some species, such as the hummingbird, have a remarkably high rate of metabolism, necessitating constant eating to remain alive. The survival advantage of having such a slow metabolism is that tortoises have been known to survive for up to one year without eating or drinking. Their slow metabolism also explains their long life expectancy. One tortoise that was presented to the queen of Tonga by English explorer Captain James Cook during the 1770s lived until 1966.

Regardless of their ability to adapt to many habitats, Galápagos tortoises are the most endangered species on the islands. Three tortoise species are known to have become extinct during the 1900s, and a fourth has a population of one and will become extinct when that lone survivor dies. There are a number of reasons for the unfortunate plight of these reptiles. One reason why several species of tortoises remain in danger of extinction is because females lay only two to sixteen eggs per year. This is a low rate compared to a sea turtle, which may lay six hundred eggs annually. A second reason relates to their longevity. Although they may live for two hundred years, this longevity means that they do not reach sexual maturity until they are quite old, and many die before they are able to reproduce.

necks upward and backward without hitting the carapace. Saddlebacks also evolved long necks to assist in reaching branches three to four feet off the ground. The saddleback-shaped shell also acts as a cooling system, allowing breezes to circulate around their bodies to lower their body temperatures. Herpetologists also report that saddleback tortoises stand high up on their legs during midday heat to increase drafts of cooling air under their shells.

The other species, the domed tortoises, evolved in moist microclimates where abundant leafy plants and grasses grow close to the ground. Their carapaces have no notch, extending very close to the backs of their necks, because these animals forage with their heads down and are able to find plenty of vegetation on the ground. For this same reason, the domed tortoises did not evolve long necks needed to reach vegetation high off the ground. Herpetologists also report that, unlike saddle-backs, domed tortoises do not stand high up on their legs because the cooler microclimates in which they thrive makes this behavior unnecessary.

The Galápagos iguanas

The microclimates also play a role in the biodiversity among Galápagos iguanas. Second only to the Galápagos tortoise, the iguanas are the most biodiverse land animals, with two different species and seven subspecies. What makes their biodiversity so remarkable is that one species lives exclusively on land while another has adapted to live both on land and in the sea.

The land iguanas exist exclusively on the islands' rough volcanic rocks. Adults average three feet in length, half of which is tail, and they weigh about twenty-five pounds. A crest of spikes runs from their head down their spine, giving them a menacing, prehistoric look. These iguanas once roved by the tens of thousands over all the Galápagos Islands; today they are found on only three of the islands, and in small numbers. Although the iguanas have a fearsome look, they are actually timid and lazy. Content to bask in the hot sun much of the day, they will seek the shade of bushes and trees to feed and cool themselves during hot afternoons. Land iguanas were first described by Darwin as

> ugly animals, of a yellowish orange beneath, and of a brownish red colour above: from their low facial angle they have a singularly stupid appearance. They are, perhaps, of a rather less size than the marine species; but several of them weighed between ten and fifteen pounds. . . . When not frightened, they slowly crawl along with their tails and bellies dragging on the ground . . . and doze for a minute or two, with closed eyes and hind legs spread out on the parched soil.[6]

Despite their ugly, menacing look, Galápagos land iguanas are actually timid, lazy animals.

The marine iguana is the more unusual of the two species because it is the only known lizard capable of surviving in the ocean. The marine iguana evolved in microclimates along the coast, and over time it adapted by acquiring the ability to swim in the ocean to feed on algae, kelp, and small crustaceans. Similar in size to the land

Marine Iguana Adaptations

The Galápagos marine iguana has evolved more adaptations for survival than any other species on the islands. The majority of its adaptations allow it to survive in the marine environment. Because of their adaptation to the ocean, they have survived better than any other Galápagos land animal, with a population throughout all of the islands of between two and three hundred thousand.

Marine iguanas have vertically flat tails that they use in a whipping motion to propel them through the water, and all four of their feet are partially webbed for the same purpose. Although they warm themselves on the rocks, they feed exclusively on seaweed in cold, shallow waters. Capable of holding their breath for up to one hour, they have been seen as deep as fifty-five feet.

Modern biologists who have performed detailed analyses of the marine iguana have discovered additional survival techniques of the species. It is the only known air-breathing animal capable of drinking saltwater as a normal part of its diet. The marine iguana possesses a salt filtration system that removes the salt from its blood, depositing it in sacks behind the eyes. When the salt sacks are full, the iguana excretes the salt through its nostrils in a sneezing action. When threatened, they will sneeze salt to ward off aggressive predators.

Iguanas are cold-blooded animals whose body temperatures are determined by their immediate surroundings. Their temperature must be kept high to remain active, and when they plunge into the cold ocean, their temperature plummets quickly. To avoid dropping to dangerously low temperatures, they have adapted the ability to survive for long periods in the cold water by shunting blood away from their body surface to conserve heat and by drastically reducing their heart rates to conserve oxygen on deep dives.

Marine iguanas have also developed longer claws than the land species to help them cling to rocks while feeding and avoid being dislodged by violent waves. When exiting the water on to volcanic rock, their long claws also assist them in gripping and scrambling up the rocks where they rest and warm their bodies in the sun.

iguana, the marine species has evolved a tail and feet adapted to swimming. Darwin noticed their distinct tail and feet immediately and reported,

> Their tails are flattened sideways, and all four feet partially webbed. They are occasionally seen some hundred yards from the shore, swimming about. . . . When in the water this lizard swims with perfect ease and quickness, by a serpentine movement of its body and flattened tail—the legs being motionless and closely collapsed on its sides.[7]

The marine iguana is also a good example of a Galápagos species that has evolved to live in both the island and coastal habitats. The marine iguana is not alone in this regard. Many Galápagos species that live along the edge of the island also depend on the coastal region for their existence.

The coastal region

The coastal region lies between the lava world of the islands' interior and the underwater realm of the sea. This region is a narrow band of shoreline about 840 miles long that wraps around the coast of each island and is a permanent home for many species and a temporary home for others. Although this region is by far the smallest of the three, it is nonetheless responsible for much of the islands' biodiversity and is crucial for the survival of many species that inhabit the other two regions.

The significance of the coastal region is its function as a biological interface or buffer region that separates the island and marine regions. This narrow band is where many of the species inhabiting the island and marine regions, although they normally exist far apart, come together and interact for their mutual benefit. In this role as a sort of commons, the coastal region provides for many of the needs of the marine and land species. Without this habitat, many species would perish.

The species that make the coastal region their permanent home are primarily of four general types: invertebrates such as sponges, crabs, sea anemones, sea urchins, corals, and sea cucumbers; a variety of small reef fish; a handful of sea birds; and a small number of species of marine mammals such as seals and sea lions. The biodiversity of the coastal region is high considering its small size. Most animals living here fill one or more of the three important roles needed in the Galápagos habitat: scavengers that clean the marine waters, prey for larger species, and predators that control the populations of smaller animals.

The scavengers that clean the marine habitat play a major role in establishing and maintaining the biodiversity within the calm waters of the coastal region. Protected from high

A sea lion and marine iguana share a beach in the Galápagos Islands. The coastal region is where many different species come together and interact.

seas and rolling swells, this is the perfect habitat for marine species that have evolved into the sifters and strainers of the ocean. Marine waters can become polluted by toxins produced as bacteria consume organic matter such as the bodies of dead land and sea animals. If decaying animal matter is not eaten first, bacterial levels can become toxic, leading to the sickness and even deaths of many marine species.

Fortunately, the coastal habitat is home to a variety of scavengers that thrive in three different microclimates: coral reefs, rocky tide pools, and mud. Each of these undersea habitats is populated by different species of scavengers that clean the water in varying ways. The coral reefs, for example, are home to dozens of small reef fish and several invertebrates, including banded coral shrimps; the rocky tide pools host lobsters, crabs, sea urchins, and a variety of eels and rock fish; and the mud is home to sea cucumbers, sea snails, and sea fans.

Most of the small coastal animals that are mobile, such as crabs, lobsters, and fish, scour the floor of the sea in search of carrion that has fallen to the bottom. Once they have eaten, these creatures excrete nitrogen that feeds other nonpolluting bacteria. Other smaller invertebrates, such as sea cucumbers, sea snails, and sea stars, filter the mud and water, removing toxin-producing microorganisms.

The sandy shores of the coastal regions also play an important role in the life of the Galápagos by providing many species with a place for birthing their offspring. Seals and sea lions use the beaches as a refuge where their pups can nurse and explore the water's edge. The warm, moist sand also provides ideal nesting places for many species of birds, sea turtles, and invertebrates that deposit their eggs there.

Some of the offspring of these creatures also serve as a food source for other Galápagos species. Circling birds search for young crab and turtles, and fish living in the shallow waters make a meal of thousands of newly hatched young. Even large marine predators such as sharks approach the shallow waters, knowing that they will find seal pups to feed on.

The marine region

If some sea creatures visit the coastal habitat in search of food, even more find sustenance in the deep waters beyond the coastline of the archipelago. This region is a massive feeding ground for all manner of sea life, so it boasts a remarkable variety of biodiversity, ranging from microorganisms to many of the world's largest marine fish and mammals.

The teeming waters of the Galápagos are best known for large deepwater fish, such as the schools of shark, tuna, swordfish, and seabass. In addition to these well-known commercial fish, the waters support several dozen midsize species, such as parrotfish and damselfish, and dozens of invertebrates, such as crabs that forage the ocean floor. Three species of dolphin and seven species of whale are the full-time resident marine mammals that live in the Galápagos marine region as well.

The marine biodiversity of the Galápagos is unusually large because two ocean currents converge on the islands.

The cool waters of the Humboldt Current, which originate in the Antarctic, flow northward directly into the Galápagos, where they collide with the warm tropical currents flowing south from Central America.

The confluence of the two currents at the Galápagos deposits an extraordinarily rich mix of marine life found nowhere else. The cold current flowing north from Antarctica carries nutrient-rich waters teeming with microorganisms, prawns, shrimps, krill, jellyfish, squid, and many small species of fish. Streaming in on the warm current flowing south are many species of mollusks, marine worms, crustaceans, echinoderms, and dozens of tropical fish species.

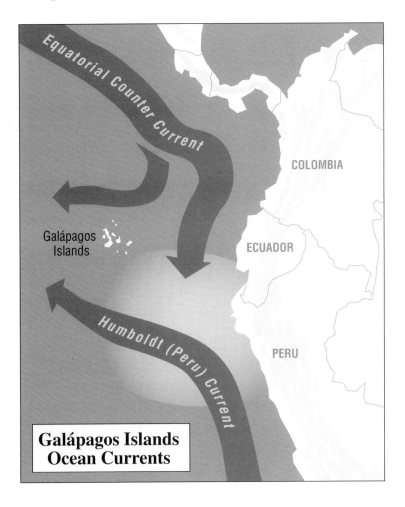

Equatorial Counter Current

COLOMBIA

Galápagos
Islands

ECUADOR

Humboldt (Peru) Current

PERU

**Galápagos Islands
Ocean Currents**

These two currents provide a gift of food for the large fish and mammals that occupy the highest links on the Galápagos marine food chain. Marine biologists refer to these steady streams of food as Galápagos soup because of their rich nutritive content for large fish. The biodiversity among these large fish is usually high because so many different food sources come in on these currents. In addition, the specimens among these predator species grow to unusually large sizes: favored commercial fish such as sharks, tuna, and swordfish can easily exceed several hundred pounds.

The large commercial fish have equally large appetites, which require tons of smaller fish daily. Michael Deal, a marine biologist and phytoplankton specialist with the University of California in Santa Barbara, explains that the food chain of the large deep-sea fish begins with microorganisms called phytoplankton. Deal explains that the phytoplankton are eaten by small fish such as anchovies and mackerel, which in turn are eaten by the large deep-sea

A Galápagos sea lion searches for food in the islands' coastal waters. Two major ocean currents flow into the Galápagos and bring an incredibly rich supply of marine life to the waters around the islands.

species. Deal estimates that a 250-pound fish must annually consume approximately 10,000 pounds of anchovies and mackerel to sustain its weight. The 10,000 pounds of anchovies and mackerel must, in turn, consume about 100,000 pounds of phytoplankton—all to sustain one fish at the top of the food chain.

The rich biodiversity of the marine region eventually contributes to the food chain for the majority of species in all three Galápagos habitat regions. Some of the smaller marine species find their way to the coastal region while some of the larger coastal species venture out to the marine region to forage.

The gift of isolation

Although the richness of the food supply contributes to the success of both plants and animals in the Galápagos, the islands' endemic species are also successful because of millions of years of evolution with little interference from foreign species. Isolated six hundred miles from the mainland of South America, hundreds of Galápagos plants and land animals established a natural balance that was not interrupted until the arrival of significant numbers of humans only two hundred years ago.

Contemporary biologists say that the isolation of the Galápagos has proven to be a gift of immeasurable value for its native species. Although the islands were discovered by Europeans in 1535, their flora and fauna have the unique distinction of having developed a multitude of species undisturbed by humankind until the nineteenth century. Subject to nothing more than the vagaries of nature, the vegetation and animals found there have had the opportunity to develop a delicate and harmonious ecological system.

The first visitor who understood the significance of the islands' isolation was Charles Darwin, who recorded the following observations: "Separated from that continent [South America] by an open space of ocean, between 500 and 600 miles in width, the archipelago is a little world within itself."[8]

The Voyage of the *Beagle*

The significance of the Galápagos Islands and their unique biodiversity would not be as well known today were it not for the voyage that Charles Darwin made on the ship HMS *Beagle*. On December 27, 1831, the HMS *Beagle*, a ten-gun British warship under the command of Captain Fitzroy, sailed from Devonport, England, on an expedition to survey the South American territories of Patagonia and Tierra del Fuego. On board was twenty-two-year-old Darwin, an aspiring naturalist whose job was to collect species and make observations about, and report on, all geologic, animal, and plant findings of interest.

On September 15, 1835, after nearly four years of traversing the Atlantic and surveying dozens of locations, the most famous person ever to visit the Galápagos, Darwin, set foot on the islands' volcanic rock. For the next five weeks Darwin wandered the seeming desolate islands, sketching the flora and fauna and taking copious notes that would later become his book *The Voyage of the "Beagle."* Darwin also collected many species that he killed and packed in trunks for further detailed examination after returning home.

Unlike those before him, Darwin noticed slight yet distinct differences within various Galápagos species. As he wandered from island to island, he closely examined tortoises, iguanas, and finches, noting in his journal that each subspecies was clearly related to other subspecies yet differed from island to island.

After the *Beagle* left the Galápagos, it continued west across the Pacific, visiting many South Pacific islands, including Tahiti, New Zealand, and Australia. As had been the case on the Galápagos, Darwin continued collecting species and writing his observations in his journal.

After the *Beagle* returned to England in 1836, Darwin collected his notes from the voyage and began to ponder the small variances that he had found in the many animal species he had observed and collected while at the different Galápagos islands. He wondered why tortoises would have slightly different shaped carapaces, why iguanas had different tails, and why finches had different beaks. These slight differences troubled Darwin.

Based on observations made during his five-year voyage on the *Beagle*, Darwin spent the remainder of his life formulating ideas about the origins of species and why some seem to flourish while others become extinct. Many modern scientists believe that had Darwin not made his visit to the Galápagos on the *Beagle* and published his book describing the voyage, the Galápagos Islands might not be as well preserved as they are today.

Since Darwin's visit, many scientists studying the wildlife of the Galápagos have recognized the good fortune of the islands' isolation from humans until such relatively late dates as the sixteenth century, thousands of years later than Europe, the Americas, and China. Spared the tampering of humans until relatively recently, the Galápagos are regarded by modern ecologists as one of the most pristine habitats on Earth.

Populating the Galápagos

The unique biodiversity found on the Galápagos is partly a function of chance. One of the many questions pondered by biologists is how the incredible array of Galápagos animals and plants found their way to this remote archipelago in the first place. Why they ask, did some species find a home here while others did not? Although biologists have many theories about how some species arrived, they have problems explaining others.

The marine currents probably carried the majority of species to the islands. All Galápagos marine animals, such as sea lions, fur seals, and penguins, could easily swim to the islands with the help of these currents.

The question, then, is how other animals less adapted to swimming made the voyage. Rafts of matted branches tangled among other forms of vegetation are sometimes spotted by mariners hundreds of miles out to sea. Scientists have long speculated that most of the larger land animals, such as tortoises, iguanas, and terrestrial mammals, must have arrived by this method. In addition to these large animals, these rafts of flotsam may have transported delicate spiders, small insects, tiny land snails, and a variety of other small creatures. When Darwin visited the Galápagos in 1835, he observed, "It is, I think, surprising that more American [South America] species have not been introduced naturally, considering that the distance is only between 500 and 600 miles from the continent, and that . . . drift-wood, bamboos, canes, and the nuts of a palm, are often washed on the southeastern shores."[9]

Winds also played a role in populating the Galápagos. The seeds of many plants, trees, and shrubs are small and lightweight and are capable of surviving for years in dry conditions. Botanists know that some seeds are so lightweight that they can be carried aloft by winds and transported thousands of miles away. Winds, too, may have made it possible for many of the larger birds that now populate the Galápagos to make the long crossing from larger landmasses.

Birds may also have transported other species to the Galápagos. Seeds eaten by birds and carried in their gut were most certainly flown across the distance from Ecuador to be later excreted on fertile soil in the Galápagos, where they germinated. Other seeds, although inedible, could have become attached to feathers and feet and given a free ride.

Scientists do not know many details about the arrival of endemic Galápagos species. When exactly the first species arrived, how many have become extinct, and why some never took hold remain unanswerable questions. Scientists do know, however, that once a large mass of species arrived and established footholds, they eventually evolved as an interdependent community. Over hundreds of thousands of years, the evolutionary path of each species was partially determined by other island species, along with the habitats, to establish a balanced community of wildlife.

One other attribute that sets the Galápagos Islands apart is that so many of their endemic species are still largely intact. 92 percent of the endemic flora and fauna seen today are believed to have inhabited the islands thousands of years ago. However, it will require intensive research and management efforts to maintain this high survival rate because many forces are placing species and their habitats at risk of extinction.

2

Invasive Species

EONS OF RELATIVE isolation had protected the unique ecological balance of the Galápagos, but a relatively recent invasion of foreign plants and animals threatens the islands' endemic wildlife. This foreign invasion includes goats, pigs, dogs, rats, and a host of insects and plants that have already destroyed some of the endemic species and habitats. The invasive species continue to inflict damage, and their numbers are growing—even as scientists and environmentalists struggle to control and eliminate them.

Of course, the first and one of the most problematic invaders were humans. The problem began in 1535 with the discovery of the islands. Fray Tomás de Berlanga, the Spanish bishop of Panama, was exploring off the coast of Ecuador when his ship was blown off course and he found himself in the Galápagos. As the first human to set foot on the desolate islands, he named them Insulae de los Galopegos, Spanish for "Island of the Hard Shells" or "Islands of the Sea Turtles."

Not until 1795, however, did anyone write about the islands. At that time, British captain George Vancouver arrived and reported that the Galápagos were:

> the most dreary barren and desolate country I ever beheld . . .
> nothing but large Cinder [volcanic rock] without any sign of
> Verdure [green color] or vegetation . . . with Seals & Penguins in vast abundance, whilst the surface of the adjacent sea
> . . . swarmed with large Lizards swimming about in different
> directions & basking at their ease.[10]

In 1795, British naval captain George Vancouver wrote about the surprising abundance of wildlife he found on the Galápagos Islands.

Following Vancouver's report about the location and abundance of wildlife on the Galápagos, other mariners arrived at the islands, and trouble from this first invasive species worsened.

Pirates and whalers

As Spanish ships bearing captured wealth from the New World made their way back to Spain, European rivals—in particular, England—encouraged pirates in their employ to attack these Spanish treasure ships. By the beginning of the eighteenth century, the Galápagos became a base of operations for many English pirates who lived off the animals they found there.

Presumably, pirates and others stopping in the islands helped themselves to the animals living there, but the earliest reference to eating tortoises is from 1835, when Charles Darwin commented, "We lived entirely upon tortoise-meat: the breast-plate roasted with the flesh on it, is very good; and the young tortoises make excellent soup; but otherwise the meat to my taste is indifferent."[11] Gradually, news of the Galápagos Islands spread, and whalers who often put to sea for months at a time came there in search of food and water. Since the Galápagos were near migrating populations of sperm whales, they were a natural stopover for those who hunted the giant marine mammals. The whalers foraged the islands for tortoises, birds and their eggs, and iguana eggs. The tortoises were especially prized since they could be captured live and could survive for months aboard ship without water or food, serving as a source of fresh meat long after the ships had left the islands. Some ships reported taking as many as two hundred tortoises at a time and stacking them in their holds. Estimates suggest that as many as a hundred thousand tortoises may have been taken during the nineteenth century. So extreme was the pressure on tortoise populations that it caused the extinction of at least three sub-species.

However, the whalers soon tired of tortoise and wanted a greater variety of meat. With this in mind, they brought goats and pigs to the islands. Whalers intentionally re-leased several goats and pigs to graze and reproduce, in hopes they would prove to be a continuing source of meat for ship crews. Other invasive species were released by ac-cident. A few dogs escaped from their owners and made their way to the interiors of several islands. Rats managed to hitch rides ashore in the small boats sailors used to ferry themselves and provisions between ship and land.

By an ironic twist of fate, even as the goat and pig popu-lations began to multiply and thrive as food sources for whalers, the industry dwindled because of declining whale populations. As whalers departed the islands, they left be-hind the goats, pigs, rats, and dogs to fend for themselves among the endemic wildlife.

An 1850 drawing depicts the taking of a Galápagos tortoise. Nineteenth-century whalers captured the hardy tortoises and kept them aboard ship to use for food during long voyages.

Combating Invasive Plants

Invasive plants do not attract much attention from the international community of conservationists, yet their introduction has been devastating in the Galápagos. Introduced plants are a serious danger for the flora of the archipelago because aggressive species compete with native species for light, water, and nutrients.

They also produce a negative impact on the native fauna and local agricultural activity. The Charles Darwin Research Station (CDRS) has a program dedicated to this topic, which undertakes constant monitoring on farms to detect newly introduced species and to register the advance of plants already introduced. In 2001 more than 10 species not previously recorded were found, which gives a total of approximately 475 species of introduced plants in the archipelago.

To respond to this problem, the CDRS has created teams that address the distribution, ecology, and impact of these plants; the execution of activities to restore native species; and the control and eradication of introduced plants. In July 1999, for example, field work was completed in a study of areas infested by elephant grass for a project that sought to identify the possible ways to improve regeneration of native plants that were overtaken by the grass.

To control invasive plants, new methods have been developed for the ten most aggressive. The methods rely heavily on the use of various herbicides at different concentrations and methods of application. As success continues, the Galápagos National Park Service will expand the number of species slated for eradication.

Predators worse than humans

The departing whalers could not have anticipated the devastation that the animals they left behind would cause. The many endemic species that had evolved as a healthy ecological community were suddenly confronted by aggressive strangers that threatened to disrupt a balance that had lasted tens of thousands of years.

Species invasions naturally occur from time to time, but not on the scale of those introduced by the whalers. Biologists working on the Galápagos recognize that winds and ocean currents still carry small birds, insects, and seeds to the islands. Nonetheless, these occurrences are infrequent, and few invading species survive because the arriving individuals are few in number and are quickly exterminated. What the whalers caused, however, was a massive invasion of large, aggressive animals that were not easily killed by the local predators.

Although the whalers were the first to bring invasive species to the Galápagos, they were not the last. Following the departure of the whalers, Ecuadorians arrived during the early twentieth century, bringing cattle, horses, cats, and a host of plants and insects capable of attaching themselves to the fur of other animals. As more and more alien species arrived, competition for food and habitat upset the long-established balance. Conservationists did not raise warning flags until the mid–twentieth century, by which time several Galápagos species were under siege.

Some endemic species could not defend themselves against the attacks of the invaders because the harmonious natural balance that had evolved over many millennia had given rise to species that no longer needed to fear or defend themselves against predators. Miguel Pellerano, Galápagos coordinator for the World Wildlife Fund, reports,

> The most serious threats come from wild goats and pigs that threaten the food supply of the magnificent Galápagos tortoises, and rats and dogs that eat the eggs of birds and reptiles that have lived without natural predators since the beginning of time.[12]

As a consequence, the numbers of invasive species surviving today total more than 800, including 475 plants and 350 animal species. With this invasion, the balance of life that had operated so successfully for eons came to an end.

Rats, dogs, and pigs

Several endemic Galápagos species were helpless when confronted by the invading animals. Today, rats, dogs, and pigs pose the worst direct threat to the endemic populations of animals. Working in packs, these primarily carnivorous animals are capable of pursuing, surrounding, and killing slower moving tortoises, young iguanas, and some birds. Their reproduction rates are also higher than those of endemic species, and without any predators capable of keeping their populations in check, their numbers overpower those of endemic animals.

Cattle graze alongside two Galápagos tortoises. The introduction to the islands of foreign species like cattle, horses, pigs, and dogs has led to a drastic decrease in the tortoise population.

The Galápagos tortoises have been injured more by invasive species than by any other animal. Slow moving and lacking any aggressive capabilities, they have proven vulnerable to the attacks of rats and dogs. When humans first arrived on the islands, the estimated number of tortoises was about two hundred thousand. Whalers killed thousands, but even after the end of whaling, the tortoises' numbers continued to decrease because of feral animal attacks. Today, following three hundred years of infestation of the islands by foreign species, the tortoise species have dwindled to about fifteen thousand, a loss of roughly 93 percent of their original population. Of the original fifteen different subspecies of the Galápagos tortoise, three are now extinct, and a fourth has but one known remaining survivor, which means that for this subspecies, extinction is inevitable.

Iguanas have also suffered. In 1978 researchers witnessed an incident in which wild dogs on Santa Cruz Island killed more than five hundred iguanas in a single attack. Similar losses have occurred on Isabela Island. Dogs, working in packs, prefer preying on the younger iguanas but can and do kill large ones as well.

The iguanas are not threatened by dogs on every island, but researchers are still concerned about the dangers posed not just by dogs but by cats as well. Martin Wikelski, a scientist working on the Galápagos, notes, "The major problems for marine iguanas are introduced feral cats and dogs. Fortunately, they only occur on some islands, so other iguana populations will not be affected. Nevertheless, these feral cats and dogs should be controlled."[13]

Direct attack from invading species on adult animals is not the only threat. Dogs and pigs are also diggers capable of smelling and digging up the eggs of tortoises, marine turtles, and iguanas that are incubating in the warm sand and dirt. As a result, survival rates for the sea turtle eggs have dropped in some years to as low as 3 percent—down from 80 percent in normal times. Dogs are also known to prey on young tortoises as well as on newly hatched land and marine iguanas. They also consume the eggs of several species of birds that nest on the ground. Furthermore, the mature individuals among flightless birds such as penguins and cormorants are also prey for dogs.

The rat infestation is wreaking a similar devastation. Rats are smaller than dogs, yet they prey on the hatchlings. On occasion, rats working in packs attack old and infirm adults as well. Researchers working for the Charles Darwin Foundation report,

> Feral rats . . . preyed on the hatchlings with nearly one hundred percent efficiency. They would also attack the giant tortoises if advantageous. In 1964, approximately 7,000 to 9,000 tortoises hatched on Pinzón Island; however ten years later, no juveniles could be found. It is believed that they were eaten by the introduced black rats.[14]

Goats

As destructive as the carnivores have been, biologists working in the Galápagos do not consider them to be the worst of the invading animals. This distinction they reserve for the goats. Habitat degradation caused by goats has indirectly led to the deaths of more plant, reptile, and bird species than all of the attacks by dogs, rats, and pigs combined. The goats are feral and have been able to invade all island habitats to graze on vegetation needed by tortoises, birds, and iguanas. Besides their voracious appetites, goats trampling the islands are altering habitats by compacting the soil, destroying plant life, and changing the water tables on several islands.

The reason goat grazing is so destructive to the endemic species is because the goats have a penchant for nipping a plant down to the ground, often pulling it out by the roots, and thus killing the plant in the process. This type of foraging leaves nothing behind for other animals. As a result, entire tracts of land are denuded of vegetation until the next spring's rain. Goats are also able to eat dry grasses, twigs, and even some types of cactus—the favored foods of the Galápagos tortoise.

The destruction of plant life leads to irreversible damage to the habitat. The goats' foraging leaves barren land that is vulnerable to soil erosion during the winter months. Although heavy rain is rarely a part of the climactic conditions on the islands, it does occasionally occur. When rain falls on sloping land that lacks plant roots to hold the dirt in place, the rushing water erodes the topsoil, cutting ravines through the land all the way to the sea. The water carries away any nutrient-rich topsoil needed by plants, leaving the hills open to still further erosion. When repeated erosion occurs, vegetation may not return for many decades, causing a loss of food sources for Galápagos tortoises as well as nesting sites for several species of birds and insects.

Cascading topsoil that spills into shallow coastal waters raises havoc with marine life. Invertebrates living on the bottom of shallow pools and marine iguanas that feed on shallow-lying seaweed experience habitat degradation as a result. Slow-moving crustaceans, such as sea cucumbers, sea urchins, and several species of mollusks, have disappeared from some locations because of mud washing into coastal shallows. Over time, the cleansing action of the waves will flush out the soil, but if the disruption recurs frequently, many species will permanently vacate the degraded habitats.

Without any natural predators, the goats' numbers grow quickly. In turn, increasingly large tracts of vegetation that were previously reserved for foraging tortoises and nesting birds are affected by overgrazing. As tortoises are forced to wander farther from their usual habitats to find food, many become dehydrated and are weakened by a lack of nourishment. Although tortoises can exist for long periods without water, they eventually succumb to dehydration during the hot Galápagos summer.

Men load goats onto a raft on the Galápagos island of Santa Cruz. Because of the destruction they wreak on the habitat, goats are the single biggest threat to the islands' endemic plant and animal species.

Some tortoises do manage to find their way to habitats that the goats have yet to attack. The tortoises that successfully migrate away from the goats face yet another problem. Depending on the microclimate, temperatures in nesting areas can differ by many degrees. Temperature variations concern herpetologists because the gender of tortoise hatchlings can be determined by the temperature at which the eggs are incubated. For example, a difference of just five degrees can result in far more males than females being hatched. If there is a sudden increase of one gender of hatchlings while the other decreases, the imbalance could be detrimental to the entire tortoise population living in that area. Researchers working for the Charles Darwin Research Station report, "Destruction of nesting zones in some areas may result in a skewing of sex ratios or total reproductive failure at specific altitudinal belts."[15]

Insects

Although goats, rats, pigs, and dogs wreak havoc on the Galápagos landscape, smaller, less noticeable insect invaders are also disrupting the ecosystem. Invasive insects initially escaped notice until they became established and nearly impossible to eradicate. Although they are small and may seem to be of little consequence compared to goats, rats, and dogs, insects play a prominent role in nature's balance on the Galápagos.

All endemic insect species are an important food source for other insects, reptiles, coastal fish, and birds. In addition to the adults, the insects' eggs and newly hatched larvae provide a vital link in the Galápagos food chain. These insects may be tiny, but with an estimated one thousand species of insects on the islands, their individual body weights of less than one gram adds up to many tons of food collectively.

The other important role insects play is as pollinators of the plants and flowers on the islands. As several species of insects move from flower to flower collecting nectar, they unwittingly also pick up and carry pollen from flower to flower, thereby serving as fertilizing agents. Without insects to perform pollination, many of the endemic flowers and plants would die. Such a disaster would, in turn, threaten the existence of herbivores that depend on them as a source of food. Without insects, maintaining the current levels of biodiversity in the Galápagos would be impossible.

Entomologists have uncovered disturbing facts about several endemic insect species, including bees. Because bees have lived on the islands for so long with only birds as predators, they have not evolved defense mechanisms to ward off other insects. For example, the Galápagos stingless bee lost its stinger thousands of years ago. Recently, a species of wasp has been introduced to the Galápagos. It is not known how it arrived, but with many cargo ships carrying fresh food from South America, ecologists speculate that it probably was among some fruit products. The wasp is aggressive and has been seen on many islands. Entomologists have observed it killing and eating the stingless bees. As the population of stingless bees declines, botanists fear their ability to pollinate flowers will also decline, leading to fewer plants that are a source of food for several land species.

Other insects threaten much larger animals directly. Fire ants, aptly named for the burning stings they inflict, have also invaded the islands. Although they have long been known as aggressive pests in many parts of the world, they are new to the Galápagos. It is widely believed that the ants emigrated from their native Central and South America mainly aboard large transport ships. Fire ants have been compared with weeds because they thrive in a wide range of climatic and geographic conditions and can spread quickly, overrunning local habitats.

Although the ecological ramifications of fire ants' presence on the Galápagos are not entirely known, early indications

Able to thrive in a range of different climates and resistant to insecticides, fire ants are an unwelcome and deadly invasive species.

have been frightening. James P. Gibbs, an environmental scientist at the State University of New York College of Environmental Science and Forestry in Syracuse, reports,

> On the Galápagos Islands, fire ants eat the hatchlings of tortoises. They have also attacked the eyes and cloacae of the adult reptiles. It's rather hideous. . . . Fire ants have reportedly taken over areas where incubator birds lay their eggs, and locals say the insect's venomous stings have blinded dogs. It's a disaster there. . . . When these invasive ants come in, they change everything.[16]

In addition, once entrenched, fire ants are extremely difficult to dislodge because they are capable of feeding on both plants and animals. Even insecticides such as Dieldrin, which is much more toxic than DDT, have failed to eradicate the pests.

Plants

The invasion of the Galápagos is not limited to animals. Foreign plants also play a significant role in the destruction of the islands' habitats. Plants can be as harmful as animals when competing for limited resources, such as water and soil nutrients. Tortoises, iguanas, and various bird species require specific plants for food, nesting grounds, and seclusion from predators. When these plants are crowded out by foreign species, the animals suffer because they will not substitute the invasive plants for the endemic ones.

Fears regarding invasive plants rose during the mid-1990s when botanists employed by the Galápagos National Park Service (GNPS) and the Charles Darwin Research Station (CDRS) initiated the Native Plants Program to investigate the status of threatened endemic flora. Following an islandwide survey, several foreign plants were identified as major threats to the natural flora. The first identified was the cinchona tree, which was introduced by the U.S. Army during World War II. The bark of the cinchona was used by the military as source of quinine, the drug that cures malaria, and the army, wanting to build an airstrip on Isabela Island, needed a ready source of this vital medicine. Effective treatments for malaria have since been developed, but now the tree grows like a weed. None of the endemic animals can eat it, and the tree crowds out native species that are food for the local animals. During an interview, Evan Rodriguez, an employee of the GNPS, pointed out a patch of native shrub called miconia, which is favored by the tortoises: "This species of Miconia is found nowhere else in the world, and we can see that the quinine [cinchona trees] below us is starting to infiltrate and take over. Unless it's stopped, this rare plant will be crowded out of existence."[17]

Conventional herbicides that kill indiscriminately—including useful plants—are not the answer. According to Tom Larson, head of environmental programs at the CDRS: "At last count, it [cinchona] covered 9,000 acres of

 Volcanic Origins

Much of the biodiversity found on the Galápagos is the result of the islands' volcanic origin. Vulcanologists believe the Galápagos Islands are the product of mantle plumes, which are columns of hot rock, roughly fifty miles in diameter, that rise from deep within the earth. These plumes, which are about fourteen hundred degrees centigrade, rise because they are hotter than the surrounding rock and are therefore less dense.

As plumes near the surface, they begin to melt. The melting occurs as a result of decompression—the decrease in pressure experienced by the plume as it rises, rather than heating. Melting probably begins at a depth of ninety miles or so and continues until the plume is prevented from further rise by the overlying lithosphere, which is the cool and rigid outer layer of the earth.

But as the hot plume rises, it eventually becomes trapped in large pools, called magma chambers, at depths between one and five miles beneath the surface. Occasionally, the magma in the chamber is able to force its way to the surface, producing a volcanic eruption. Successive eruptions over millions of years have produced the Galápagos Islands. Vulcanologists estimate that the oldest plumes are about 90 million years old.

Over time, the lava decomposed and mixed with soils to develop rich nutrients for plant life and the perfect habitat for desert animals. Today, many species of drought-resistant plants flourish across the stark volcanic landscape. Joining the plants are several species of reptiles and birds that thrive in lava-rock environments where they can lay their eggs and have them incubate among the volcanic crevices.

Guava trees were introduced to the islands by Ecuadorian farmers. They now cover twenty thousand acres of land and are crowding out native plant species.

park land, and it's been spreading at a furious pace. Biologists from the Czech Republic are trying to develop an injectable poison for the plants, but so far they've not had all that much success."[18]

Other major foreign threats include guava and mango trees. Both trees were brought to the Galápagos Islands by a few Ecuadorian farmers who hoped to make money on these cash crops. The farmers, however, soon found that they could not compete with growers in Central and South America and abandoned their groves, which continue to thrive and exclude native plants. The CDRS estimates that guava alone covers twenty thousand acres of land.

Stopping the spread of the fruit trees is almost impossible because a few species of birds eat the sweet fruit the trees bear. After gorging themselves on the pulpy fruit and seeds, these birds fly many miles to other islands, dropping the seeds through their excrement. When rains come, some of the seeds germinate and grow. This natural form of seed distribution has been responsible for the spread of these two trees, which strangle increasingly large numbers of native plant species needed by other birds and native land animals.

Invasive species continue to threaten the islands' endemic species and their habitats. Environmental scientists at the CDRS estimate that the Galápagos have over 500 alien species spread over more than 120 islands. Since the 1990s, they estimate that between 100 and 150 new plant species have been introduced to the islands.

In spite of these alarming rates of invasion by species, Galápagos scientists are quick to point out that invasive species are only one part of the problem. Another element is human. Fishermen flocking to the islands to exploit the rich treasure of sea life are having as dramatic and disastrous an impact as are the invasive plants and animals.

3

Fishing Threats

EXCESSIVE FISHING IN the waters around the Galápagos Islands is threatening the survival of several marine
animals that make the Galápagos their home. The problem
is twofold. Increasing numbers of fishermen are pursuing
dwindling populations of fish. Furthermore, the influx of
fishermen moving to the islands from the Ecuadorian
mainland is contributing to general environmental pollution in the islands.

The bounty of the waters of the Galápagos was not
threatened until the 1970s. Ecuadorians living on the mainland had fished the coastal waters for generations, but as
their country's population grew, so too did the tons of
seafood required to feed the people. Over the years, the
density of fish in nearby waters declined, forcing fishermen to search elsewhere for their quarry. Since international law prevented Ecuadorians from fishing the coastal
waters of neighboring South American countries, many
moved westward to look for better prospects in the relatively unfished waters of the Galápagos.

Although the Galápagos have provided new fishing
grounds, many problems have arisen as a result of the
sudden intrusion of fishermen, who have moved their
homes to the islands. Today the islands' human population has exploded from a few thousand to seventeen thousand inhabitants, most of whom are in some way involved
in the fishing industry. These people go about harvesting
the riches of the sea, but in the process they are upsetting
the ecological balance in the area. Environmental journal-

ist Monte Hayes, visiting the Galápagos in January 2001, made this observation:

> Seeking to exploit the rich waters off the islands, they [the fishermen] oppose limits on fishing for lobster and for sea cucumbers, bottom-feeding invertebrates crucial to the shallow water ecosystem. Fishermen also want freedom to hunt the Galápagos' protected sharks. Sea cucumbers and shark fin fetch astronomical prices in Asia, where they are prized as aphrodisiacs.[19]

Pelagic fishing

More than simply the inhabitants of the coastal waters are under pressure. The pelagic fishing grounds, those in deep waters that lie many miles off the coast of the Galápagos, are home to schools of large fish species, including tuna, marlin, shark, and swordfish. Although local Galápagos fishermen used traditional fishing rods and reels—which allowed them to catch only one fish at a time—they were able to catch enormous numbers of these species.

The success of the local fishermen, however, soon became their curse. As news of their record-breaking prized

Fishermen haul in tuna near the Galápagos Islands in the 1950s. Not until the 1970s did excessive fishing begin to threaten the ecological balance of the islands' coastal waters.

catches spread from port to port, large foreign fleets of boats equipped for large-scale harvesting descended on the Galápagos to grab a larger share of the catch. Rodrigo Bustamante, a marine biologist working in the Galápagos, made this observation of the problem in 1998:

> Industrial fishing boats come from mainland Ecuador and abroad to fish for shark and tuna. In recent years the total fishing pressure, of all kinds, has increased rapidly, with large numbers of long-liners visiting the islands. In addition, the 1990s saw a sudden rush for tuna and shark that brought in its wake environmental damage, and resource depletion. . . . It is clear to everyone in Galápagos, including the local fishermen, that returns are diminishing and that effective management of the marine area is needed.[20]

Fishermen who intentionally concentrate on some species of large pelagic fish but not on others damage more than the just the pelagic environment. This practice has a cascading effect that also adversely impacts coastal shallow water species and some on land as well. When some pelagic species decline and others do not, the balance between predator and prey fish is upset; this, in turn, upsets balances throughout all of the Galápagos.

Nature's predator-prey relationship is complex and constantly shifting. Sometimes, for example, an abundance of prey fish allows predators such as sharks to overbreed and eventually the prey populations are reduced to very low numbers. As the prey supply declines, the sharks face starvation. The resulting decline among predators in time allows the prey populations to gradually recover. This naturally occurring cyclical pattern results in a delicate balance between predator and prey.

Recent human intervention, however, has upset this natural predator-prey cycle. If fishermen continue to decimate shark populations, the loss of this top marine predator may trigger a cascade of disruptions throughout all Galápagos habitats. If the cycle becomes too imbalanced, recovery may become impossible.

A sudden shark shortage, should it occur, could affect the coastal region. Two of the favorite foods of sharks—besides other fish—are the seals and sea lions that live in

Finning

Sharks depend on both their teeth and multiple sets of fins for survival. Tragically, shark fins are valued in Asian cultures as the primary ingredient in shark fin soup, which is savored as a delicacy. In 2000 a worldwide organization called TRAFFIC, which tracks the illegal and unethical sale of animal parts, published *An Overview of World Trade in Sharks and Other Cartilaginous Fishes.* This report which appears at TRAFFIC's website www.traffic.org/factfile/factfile_sharks.html, states "In Hong Kong, the world capital of shark fin cuisine, retail prices generally range as high as $564 per kilo [$256 per pound], while a bowl of shark fin soup can sell for up to $90." Shark fins are now among the world's most expensive fisheries products, although the value varies according to color, size, thickness, and fin gelatin content.

The high price for shark fin soup is placing the shark's survival in jeopardy off the coast of the Galápagos. Commercial fishing ships from Asian nations patrol the Galápagos in search of sharks—not for their value as food but rather for their fins. When sharks are caught and hauled out of the water, in a process known as "finning," fishermen slice off the fins and throw the live shark back in the water. Stunned and unable to swim, they die a grisly death, either being eaten by other sharks or from a lack of oxygen because, without fins, they cannot push water through their gills.

Sharks are illegally killed for their fins, which are highly valued as a delicacy in some Asian cultures.

the coastal habitat. If the shark population declines, the seal and sea lion populations will increase and exert pressure on their primary food sources, which are small coastal fish and crustaceans, such as shrimps and crabs. If these small animals are eaten in unusually large numbers, they will not be able to reproduce fast enough to keep up with the seal and sea lion populations; as a result, they—along with the sharks—will become threatened.

High-tech fishing

The recent depletion of large numbers of shark and other pelagic fish species is the result of new high-tech fishing techniques practiced by foreign fishing industries. Large, modern commercial fishing boats, primarily from Asia, are responsible for the recent depletion of many pelagic species. These boats are several hundred feet long and function as floating processing plants capable of catching, cleaning, cutting, and freezing the fish.

The fleets of foreign fishing boats that are capable of traveling thousands of miles to the Galápagos have developed high-tech fishing methods capable of large-scale capture. The objective for the owners of these large boats is to fill their holds as quickly as possible, speed back to port to unload the catch, and return to fishing with the least amount of unproductive time in port.

Marine biologists in the Galápagos are concerned about the use of two new large-scale, high-tech fishing methods that are being used to fill the foreign boats: long-line and drift-net fishing. The objective of each method is the same—to catch the largest possible number of fish in the shortest possible time.

Long-line fishing utilizes a steel cable, sometimes forty miles long, that is attached to buoys to prevent it from sinking to the ocean's floor. Attached to the steel line every fifty feet are ten-foot-long nylon fishing lines called "drop lines," each of which has a baited hook. A fishing boat plays out the long line and its thousands of drop lines into the water and drags it behind the boat for several hours. As it slowly moves through the water, schools of fish attracted

to the chunks of bait strike the hooks. When a fish takes the baited hook, it fights to exhaustion against the weight of the heavy main cable and the floats. When the captain sees that the lines are nearly full, the ship winches in the cable and collects the catch. By employing this process, many tons of fish can be taken very quickly.

Drift nets are a net system made of synthetic fibers that are nearly invisible, are very flexible, and are capable of entangling any animal larger than its mesh. The drift nets, often up to sixty miles in length and one hundred yards wide, are released from the fishing boats and are designed to drift suspended in the water like a sixty-mile-long underwater fence. The drift nets are set at night to avoid being seen by fish. In the morning, they are retrieved along with everything they have entangled.

Schools of Galápagos tuna have been decimated by the drift nets, as have shark, marlin, and swordfish. Drift nets are now banned by most nations, but it is such a lucrative way to catch fish that many fishing boat captains flout the

Fishermen drop their nets into the waters off the islands. Such small-scale fishing does not pose as much of a threat to local fish populations as large, commercial operations that use drift nets and long lines.

law. The effect on many pelagic species has been devastating. Roger Payne, a professor of marine biology who works in the Galápagos, explains why fish populations have declined so dramatically:

> The pattern that has emerged from the vast majority of fisheries studies in every major fishery from all over the world is that rather than predators like whales being the problem, it is almost always human fishing practices that cause the big depletions of fish stocks.[21]

If the current levels of fishing continue, conservationists believe the populations of several pelagic species will drop below sustainable levels and will die out altogether, forever altering the balance of the deep-sea habitat.

A tragic slaughter

The long lines and drift nets that weave a web around the Galápagos kill many unintended victims as well. These fishing techniques indiscriminately catch every type of marine animal without regard for its commercial value or importance to the ocean's ecology. As increasing numbers of long lines and drift nets are used in the waters of the Galápagos, the threat of extinction to untargeted species grows.

A diver attempts to free a shark that has become entangled in fishing lines.

The thousands of baited hooks on the long lines that float through the water and near the surface snare more than fish. Sea birds, especially albatross and frigates, that fly high above the water, can see the chunks of bait but not the hooks. These sea birds dive into the water to grab what appears to be a quick meal only to be snagged and drowned on the end of a hook. In 1998 the Galápagos National Park Service (GNPS) received reports from fishermen of twenty to thirty boobies being killed each day along with albatross and other large marine birds. Galápagos sea turtles and small seals and sea lions suffer the same fate as the birds. Environmental journalist Andrea Dorfman reports, "The number of critically endangered turtles . . . has more than doubled. Among birds, the number of threatened albatrosses jumped from 3 to 16 [species], owing to long line fishing."[22]

The same sorts of grisly deaths occur in drift nets. Invisible during the night to marine animals, the nets entangle swimming turtles and mammals. Unable to free themselves to swim to the surface, they drown. According to the management coordinator of the GNPS, Pippa Heylings,

> These areas are of vital importance as feeding grounds for the flagship species in Galápagos, such as sea lions, frigates, albatross etc. These areas, however, were well known to fishermen—especially the industrial fishermen—who were fishing with long-lines and nets which are notorious for their destruction of these key species.[23]

Even worse, entire drift nets are sometimes lost by boats and end up far from where they were set, killing even more unintended victims for months after breaking loose.

Tragically, many fish and other animals killed so needlessly simply go to waste. Some of the boats in search of only one species of fish, such as tuna or swordfish, will throw overboard all other unwanted species, called "by-catch," which are often already dead. In these waters, by-catch includes dozens of species of important fish as well as marine mammals and marine turtles. Regarding the discard of dead shark by-catch, marine biologists working at the Pelagic Shark Rescue Foundation report,

In addition to being directly targeted in various commercial and recreational fisheries throughout the world, sharks are all too often captured incidentally as by-catch in tuna and billfish [swordfish] fisheries. Shark by-catch in large-scale high-seas fisheries around the world could be as much as 50% of the reported catch. . . . In many cases this by-catch is discarded.[24]

The loss of large numbers of shark affects more that just the predator-prey cycle. Sharks also play an important role as scavengers of the deep seas. Most people do not realize that much of what sharks eat is carrion—the decaying carcasses of dead fish and mammals. If dead animals are not eaten, they decay and produce large concentrations of bacteria that may cause sickness and even death if ingested by other marine species. Sharks, then, serve as cleaning machines of the ocean. In an interview with Jerry T. Goldsmith, the curator at San Diego's Sea World, Goldsmith notes, "If the shark populations diminish, lots of dead fish will decay in the ocean causing a potentially serious contamination problem."[25]

Another benefit that is being lost as sharks disappear is their medicinal value to humans. Several medicines and food products are produced from the cartilage of sharks. Chondrichthyan natrium, a chemical compound found in shark cartilage, is used to treat eye fatigue and rheumatism. Shark liver oil is useful for things such as vitamin supplements and blood anticlotting compound. A chemical extracted from shark cartilage has also been successfully used to develop a synthetic skin for burn victims. And in recent years, shark cartilage powder and capsules have been marketed extensively as a product purporting to assist in the treatment of some cancers.

Not all dangers to marine life lurk in the darkness of the sea. Tourist beaches that are lit at night by artificial lights attract hatchling sea turtles that become disoriented, causing them to crawl toward the lights rather than toward the sea. Marine biologists explain that in the wild, turtles emerge from their sandy nests and await the moon or sun as it moves across the night sky. However, when hotel and restaurant lights are bright at night, the baby turtles get confused and head away from the water. Although conser-

El Niño

Humans are responsible for most of the species endangerment in the Galápagos, but not all of them. During the winter of 1997–1998, an oceanic and atmospheric phenomenon in the Pacific Ocean known as El Niño increased the ocean temperature several degrees higher than normal. This temperature rise reduced the density of marine species around the islands and changed climatic conditions, all of which significantly affected the wildlife of the Galápagos.

The warmer-than-usual waters caused a sudden growth explosion of plankton, which marine biologists blame for choking off essential ocean nutrients that usually are brought to the Galápagos by deep, cold, upwelling currents. The lack of nutrients essentially starves the entire ecosystem, beginning with the microscopic phyloplankton and extending all the way to the top of the food chain—marine mammals.

Nearly all major animals were affected in one way or another by the dramatic climate change. The Charles Darwin Foundation studied sea lions and found that the principal colonies in central and southern Galápagos declined in number by an average of 48 percent. Many sea lions migrated away, and there was also high mortality due to starvation.

Even the tortoises suffered. Heavier-than-normal rains pelted the islands, saturating the soil used for nesting. Female tortoises successfully located patches of soil for nesting, but soil temperatures decreased due to increased moisture and shading from flourishing vegetation. Though nesting sites were relatively well drained, a high level of egg mortality was associated with heavy rains and unusual temperatures. Experimental data strongly suggested that El Niño rains resulted in near total reproductive failure at many tortoise nesting sites.

Fortunately for the plants and animals of the Galápagos, researchers are now reporting normal marine conditions and the return to normalcy for the local wildlife.

vationists try to help them reach the breaking waves, some become targets for marine birds, dogs, and rats, which pick them up and eat them.

The plight of sea turtles has been studied and publicized since the 1970s, when environmentalists judged all seven species on the Galápagos to be endangered. Although progress has been made in protecting baby sea turtles at some of their best-known nesting grounds, illegal poaching for meat and eggs remains a widespread problem. Moreover, newly hatched sea turtles continue to suffer inadvertent, but significant, mortality from small mesh nets set for fish and shrimp.

Coastal fishing

The shallow coastal waters of the Galápagos are also experiencing ecological destruction resulting from fishing pressure. Even more than pelagic species, marine life in the shallow waters close to the islands is in a precarious position. Although there are over three hundred species of fish around the Galápagos, the echinoderms—sea cucumbers, sea urchins, and sea stars—and the crustaceans—crabs, lobsters, shrimps, and barnacles—are attracting most of the concern of marine biologists.

Although sea cucumbers in the Galápagos did not arouse much interest among biologists in the past, scientists now are concerned for their rapid population decline. The loss of these relatively obscure, bottom-dwelling invertebrates may have serious consequences for the survival of other species that are part of the same complex food chain.

The story of the sea cucumber illustrates how distant events can directly impact the health of an entire species in the Galápagos. Interest in Galápagos sea cucumbers was almost nonexistent until Asian importers visited the islands in 1988 and began buying them because they are considered delicacies by many Asians, who also value them as aphrodisiacs. The coming of the Asian importers to the Galápagos sent the price of sea cucumbers up dramatically. Seemingly overnight, hundreds of fishermen saw an opportunity to get rich fast and began harvesting sea cucumbers by the ton until the GNPS became concerned. To balance the rights of the fishermen to earn a livelihood yet protect sea cucumbers from extinction, catch limits were imposed for the first time.

In October 1994 the GNPS allowed fishermen a three-month season during which a quota of 550,000 sea cucumbers was set. The biologists employed by the park believed this number would not endanger the species. Around eight hundred fishermen began collecting sea cucumbers within the Galápagos marine reserve under the watchful eye of the GNPS. Unfortunately, the fishermen disregarded orders to cease harvesting once the limit was reached and exceeded the established limit, collecting somewhere between 6 and

The overfishing of Galápagos sea cucumbers became such a problem that a limit was placed on the numbers of them that could be harvested.

10 million sea cucumbers. According to this Charles Darwin Foundation news release,

> Tension following the excessive extraction of sea cucumbers ran high and continues to this day. The 2000 season reopened against scientific recommendations with 1,387 fishermen registered removing the legal quota of four and a half million sea cucumbers—about fifty-four tons—after just two months. "Continued illegal fishing is posing a threat to local sea cucumber populations and threatening to affect the unique ecosystem of the Galapagos Islands," said Teresa Mulliken, TRAFFIC [the World Wildlife Fund's wildlife trade monitoring program] Research and Network Development manager and co-author of the study. "[As a province of Ecuador] it's vital that the government of Ecuador bring the fishery and trade under more effective control and for consumer countries and others to provide assistance where they can."[26]

Such overfishing is of concern because the sea cucumber serves a vital role by filtering ocean sediments and recycling nutrients back into the food web. As they slowly move along the ocean floor, they swallow sediment and grind the organic food particles into finer particles that bacteria can then further decompose. In this process, they also help to purify the seawater. By performing this important cleaning function, they ensure the maintenance of a healthy ecosystem in the waters surrounding the Galápagos. Marine biologist David Pawson explains that sea cucumbers are the "earthworms of the sea. They feed on detritus [organic debris] and turn over the sea floor much as earthworms do on land. Like earthworms in terrestrial systems, sea cucumbers often make up 90% of the animal biomass in marine systems."[27]

Human population growth

Beyond their direct effect on marine populations, fishermen have also contributed to the decline of the Galápagos environment. The recent and sudden influx of native Ecuadorian fishermen and their families has added what might be the most intense threat to the ecology of the Galápagos Islands. Until the late twentieth century, the permanent human population was about one thousand, hardly enough to significantly impact the environment. By the late 1990s, however, the official census estimated the population to be around fifteen thousand, and by 2000 it had grown to an estimated seventeen thousand. Estimates of future population growth project an increase to forty thousand residents in 2015 and to eighty thousand by 2027.

The presence of thousands of people on such a small amount of land has created conditions that stress the delicate balances of nature. One of the problems for this burgeoning population is that 97 percent of the islands' total land mass is within the wildlife preserve area and is therefore off limits to human habitation.

Polluting shantytowns

The Galápagos are simply not equipped to accommodate the rapidly growing human population. Existing fishing villages are little more than shantytowns built of sticks and scrap sheet metal. Modern sanitation services are nonexistent. Sewers drain directly into the bays, exposing marine species to toxic bacteria and organic material. As levels of toxicity rise in lagoons near the fishing villages, crustaceans become sick, as do all animals that feed on them. Although wave and tidal action cleans out much of the toxic bacteria, over long periods of time, these areas may cease their ability to sustain the current levels of healthy biodiversity.

Lack of adequate trash disposal worsens the impact of the exploding human population. Plastic and paper waste

Social Conflict

Sometimes disagreements between two opposing groups of people over the wildlife of the Galápagos can escalate to violence. In January 1995 local fishermen believed that their livelihoods were threatened by laws limiting the numbers of sea cucumbers and lobsters they were allowed to harvest. Defying the law, they marched inland and took over the park service and facilities operated by the Charles Darwin Research Station. They further threatened to sabotage conservation services, harm staff, and kill certain endangered species on the islands unless they were allowed to continue fishing beyond the legal limits.

When no successful resolution could be reached, a second series of violence erupted in March 1997, worse than the first. Government property was damaged and stolen, municipal property was taken over, and the staffs were prevented from working. A park warden was shot and seriously wounded by illegal fishermen while trying to inspect an illegal fishing camp and sea cucumber processing plant on the west coast of Isabela.

Violence flared for the same reasons again in November 2000. On November 22, the Association of Park Wardens of the Galápagos National Park Service sent a formal letter to the president of Ecuador, Gustavo Noboa Bejarano. In this letter, they demanded the enforcement of all fishing laws and protection for employees working on the islands. But the most dramatic statement, contained in the GNPS Annual Report for the year 2000, was the following:

> Mr. President, if by the end of this month we do not have real solutions, that are corrective and capable of being carried out, that recover, improve, and strengthen the authority of our institution and its members, and that effectively apply the laws that regulate activities in the Province of Galápagos, we will be forced to abandon the conservation activities and administration of the Terrestrial National Park and the Marine Reserve of Galápagos.

has become a problem as it blows about the islands and into the sea. The animals that are most endangered by trash are birds, marine mammals such as seals and sea lions, and marine turtles. Seals and sea lions have been found floundering in the surf with their heads caught in plastic containers, and a few have washed up on beaches strangled by plastic objects around their necks. Marine turtles, mistaking clear plastic bags floating in the surf for their favorite food, jellyfish, choke to death trying to swallow the bags.

Living in undeveloped towns without electricity means that all cooking and heating is done on open wood-burning

A village on the island of San Cristóbal. Human population growth on the islands has placed a strain on the islands' ecosystem.

stoves. Wood is scarce on the dry Galápagos landscape, forcing the inhabitants to harvest brush and trees that for hundreds of thousands of years have been needed for food by the tortoises, as nesting havens for birds and iguanas, and as protection for endemic insects. As increasing numbers of the local people remove trees and brush for fuel—often doing so illegally in the preserve areas—more destruction of natural habitat takes place and more species become threatened.

Some scientists portray the problem as an example of human greed. Chantal Blanton, director of the Charles Darwin Research Station on Santa Cruz Island until 1996, concludes, "The major core problem in the Galápagos right now is the burgeoning human population that has occurred. . . . It's that get-rich, short-term, gold-rush mentality which, I think, is at the core of the problems that the Galápagos is currently having."[28]

This growth of population, coupled with the effects of overfishing, has severely stressed the Galápagos ecosystem. Conservationists believe that the population has already exceeded the carrying capacity of the land allotted for human use. If population numbers continue to increase, scientists speculate that efforts by those working to conserve the natural species will be overwhelmed and more species may become extinct.

4

Ecotourism Threats

IRONICALLY, PUBLIC AWARENESS of the fragility of the Galápagos contributes to the islands' problems. The Galápagos have experienced another threat over the past thirty years as tourists descend on the islands. Eager to see the endangered reptiles, beautiful coastal marine life, and exotic collection of birds, tourists have trampled the delicate vegetation, disturbed nesting areas, and sometimes littered the islands and their waters with carelessly discarded waste. Although many tourists are sensitive to the delicate ecology of the Galápagos, nevertheless, the islands and their native species bear the environmental scars left by visitors.

The Galápagos tourist trade that began in the 1970s with about one thousand visitors a year ballooned by the year 2000 to sixty thousand. An increase of this magnitude has overstressed the resources of the islands to the point that they can no longer adequately support tourism without damaging the environment. Craig McFarland, the former director of the Charles Darwin Foundation, reports,

> Although tourism has been growing in Galápagos throughout the almost 30 years of its existence, this growth has been driven by economic interests, and neither planned technically in relation to the natural resource base, nor related to potential market studies. In fact, there is evidence that the islands cannot support tourist demand, even though there are some private sector interest groups inside and especially outside of Galápagos on continental Ecuador that would like to bring in even more vessels [cruise ships] and operators. [29]

In response to concern about the impact visitors have on environmentally threatened habitats such as the Galápagos,

A group of tourists hike past tortoises along the rim of Alcedo Volcano on Isabela Island.

a new type of vacation pastime, called ecotourism, has become popular. Ecotourism differs from conventional tourism by stressing reduced environmental impact on the sites being visited. As a rule, ecotourism emphasizes travel to remote, undeveloped areas and efforts to sustain the well-being of the native inhabitants. Optimally, ecotourism involves the use of technologies and accommodations for visitors that will not add to local pollution or threaten the local wildlife.

Still, although ecotourists tend to embrace sound environmental practices, their increased presence is threatening to change the entire character and purpose of travel to the islands. For example, in an effort to cash in on the growing demand for tours of the Galápagos, cruise-line operators are pressuring the Ecuadorian government to allow larger cruise ships to operate within the islands. Demands to increase the capacity of cruise ships from twenty passengers to four hundred are under consideration.

Some entrepreneurs, whose interests are to cater to ecotourists, have also proposed the construction of new hotels, casinos, and airstrips. Charter boat owners introduced

The Need for Ecotourism

Ecotourism, in spite of the problems it can cause to the fragile habitats of the Galápagos, is an important source of income for the local population of islanders as well as for scientific research. Neither of these two groups wants to see ecotourism entirely disappear. However, if it is not carefully controlled, ecotourism may undermine conservation efforts and destroy the successful ecotourism industry.

In the year 2000 directors of the Charles Darwin Foundation (CDF) analyzed ecotourism in the Galápagos. Specifically, they studied the impact of ecotourism on the habitats and species to determine which policies were successful and which were harmful. When they completed the analysis, they pointed out concerns that must be corrected to guarantee the continued success of ecotourism.

The analysis also identified that the major source of revenue for scientific and conservation work was funded by tourist fees. Each tourist to visit the islands pays an average of eighty dollars as an entry fee to the Ecuadorian government. Half of the fee is spent to upgrade the islands' infrastructure, improving schools, roads, sanitation, and other services. The other half is turned over to the Galápagos National Park Service (GNPS) to fund its conservation work and research. Between 1984 and 1996, 34 percent of the GNPS budget came from these tourist fees.

Scientists working for the GNPS and the CDF also understand that the Galápagos, in addition to its role as a research facility, is an educational facility. Ecotourists visiting the islands are provided with valuable presentations and lectures on conservation practices and receive information about political and social action that can be implemented to protect endangered species not only on the Galápagos but also on other fragile ecosystems around the world. If ecotourism was halted on the Galápagos, these valuable lessons—which are provided to 60,000 visitors annually—would be lost.

Visitors observe Galápagos tortoises at the Charles Darwin Research Station.

sport fishing and scuba diving to the islands for the first time in 1997, as an additional attraction for ecotourists. Furthermore, increasing numbers of less environmentally sensitive tour operators disregard the rules regarding travel across the islands and under the seas.

The tourist trade

As their numbers rise, tourists are replacing the fishing industry as the largest source of income in the Galápagos Islands. Tourism is also replacing fishing as the most destructive industry in terms of environmental damage. In spite of the desolate character of the Galápagos Islands, ecotourists, who spend thousands of dollars getting there, want many of the same luxuries found in traditional tourist locations. To accommodate them, corporations have built more than three dozen hotels over the past twenty years on the four major islands, along with restaurants, bars, and hundreds of souvenir shops. All of these amenities create forms of pollution. Some tourists find similar amenities on the more than one hundred cruise ships and yachts registered with the Galápagos National Park Service (GNPS). Just like the hotels, however, these seaborne accommodations contribute to the growing pollution problems of the islands.

Some experts believe that the problem is simply that too many people are coming to the islands. Even environmental groups that sponsor some tours are concerned about the impact of ecotourism. According to Andy Drumm, director of the Nature Conservancy's ecotourism program,

> Unregulated tourism is the threat. It's a booming industry. As the industry booms, you end up with a lot of people, and the traffic is too much for the infrastructure. The parks officials will be measuring the impact to try to determine how many people can visit each place.[30]

Tourist pollution

The care and feeding of tourists, whether they are staying on the island or on shipboard, results in the accumulation of waste that is deposited onto and into the Galápagos environment. Tourists generate tons of debris in the form

of uneaten food, food and dry goods packaging, sewage, chemicals and cleaning solutions, and a variety of incidental trash associated with all tourist facilities.

The amount of solid waste on the islands has been increasing rapidly both from tourists as well as from waste thrown into the sea from tour vessels, which then washes up on the beaches. In both cases, the accumulation creates a visual blight as well as a threat to wildlife. David Brown, a geography graduate student working on ecotourism in the Galápagos for the Galápagos Coalition, a group of scientists and lawyers interested in the relationship between conservation and human activities, made this observation:

Tourism has replaced fishing as the islands' largest source of income, but has also caused a great deal of environmental damage.

> Visual impacts are obvious in numerous places that 10–20 years ago never had any notable accumulated solid waste. Other impacts are unknown quantitatively, except that individual animals are known to be killed or severely injured in a variety of ways by solid waste: sea turtles eat plastic bags; sea lions are lacerated by metal cans and strangled by items like pulleys and fan belts.[31]

Solid waste that is dropped by tourists as well as trash generated by the tourist hotels and restaurants is collected and deposited at an open garbage dump on Santa Cruz Island. There, all combustible trash is separated and accumulated

A sea lion rests near trash washed up on a beach in the Galápagos Islands.

until enough builds up to warrant incineration. When the waste is burned, the smoke is visible through the archipelago, and the smell carries with the winds.

Although the smell and sight of the incineration is unfortunate on the designated burning days, it is not a temporary problem. According to the Environmental News Network, "Smog created by the burning is long-lasting and migrates great distances."[32]

Sewage from hotels and cruise ships is also of particular concern to coastal marine biologists. The government of Ecuador has not built any sewage treatment plants on any of the islands. This means that all sewage from ships is pumped directly into the water, and hotels and restaurants pump theirs through one-mile-long pipes into the coastal waters near the major settlements. Although the raw sewage is generally diluted as it mixes with seawater, the outfall pipes are never moved, causing a build up of bacteria near the pipe openings. The resulting high levels of toxins produced by these bacteria are causing the extermination of all invertebrates that cannot escape; these areas of poisoned water are ever widening.

Cruise ships

Many ecotourists mistakenly believe that by experiencing the Galápagos by boat, they are damaging the islands' ecology less than if they stay in hotels on the islands. But over the last decade, as tourism has soared, tour companies and boat owners catering to visitors have offered more onboard comforts, which in turn increases the pollutants that are released into the air or water. Carelessly discarded cleaning solutions used to launder clothes and to clean bathrooms are flushed into the water along with other fluid waste. As meals become more elaborate the waste associated with discarded food and food packaging grows. Even onboard evening entertainment entails the use and disposal

Tourists from larger tour boats anchored off North Seymour Island in the Galápagos arrive by panja.

of glass, plastics, and paper products. As more and more ship owners feel compelled to offer the latest amenities and entertainment, the environment will suffer. And, of course, the sheer number of vessels is growing. According to Martha Honey, who has written widely on ecotourism in the Galápagos, "There are now about one hundred yachts, cabin cruisers, and sailing vessels—almost double the number in 1987."[33]

The GNPS has intentionally avoided building docks for cruise ships because several would need to be constructed, one for each of the major islands, and each would cause considerable destruction of coastal marine environments. Without docks, however, each boat that arrives on the islands must anchor offshore before loading passengers on to small, inflatable boats called *panja,* which ferry them to shore.

Each time a multi-ton anchor is dropped, it crushes everything beneath it as it settles to the bottom. Even the small anchors used by dive boats carrying scuba divers to view colorful fish cause significant damage to delicate coral formations. This constant pounding of anchors as they hit the ocean floor, along with occasional dragging that occurs during high winds, is becoming an increasing problem for marine biologists working to preserve endangered coastal invertebrates.

Species suffering the worst habitat destruction from dropped anchors are shrimps, sea cucumbers, coral, sea urchins, and lobsters. At particular risk in the Galápagos is black coral, which is already an endangered species. Because coral grows very slowly, broken and crushed coral formations may take decades to regenerate. Scientists have requested that the government anchor permanent buoys to the ocean floor so ships can tie up to them, thereby eliminating the need to drop their anchors, but as yet, nothing has been done to make these buoys a reality.

Fueling cruise ship

The growing popularity of the cruise industry has created growing concerns about the potential for some sort of maritime disaster. The Galápagos coastline can be treacherous because of jagged volcanic rocks lying just under the sea between the many islands. Nighttime in the waters can be particularly dangerous if boat captains are unfamiliar with the channels. Furthermore, when high winds and swift currents are creating turbulent waters, even rocks that are visible constitute a real threat to boats.

The experience of the fuel tanker *Jessica* illustrates what can go wrong. On January 16, 2001, the *Jessica* was passing along San Cristóbal Island on its way to refuel the cruise ship *Galápagos Explorer*. The ship was carrying 160,000 gallons of its own diesel fuel and another 80,000 gallons of fuel intended for the *Galápagos Explorer*. At approximately ten o'clock at night, the tanker ran aground at the entry to port Baquerizo Moreno.

Coordinated action between the Ecuadorian navy and the directors of the GNPS prevented any spilling while the

After running aground, the fuel tanker Jessica *leaks oil into the ecologically sensitive waters of the Galápagos.*

vessel was towed off the rocks. The next day, however, the tanker listed to twenty-five degrees, causing a spill of about two thousand gallons of fuel. Before crews could remove the remainder of the fuel, the ship split open on the rocks and the remainder of the cargo, along with the ship's own diesel spilled into the sea.

Quick action on the part of the GNPS and naval personnel minimized the impact of the oil spill on sea life. All told, it has been calculated that between 5 and 10 percent of the bay was covered with oil and that only seven sea lions and approximately fifteen birds—both pelicans and blue-footed boobies—were affected by the fuel. Staff at the GNPS collected these animals for treatment.

For some organizations, the accident was simply confirmation of long-standing concerns. Prior to the spill, BirdLife International, a conservation group concerned with endangered birds throughout the world, had petitioned the Ecuadorian government to prohibit ships from transporting hazardous products among the Galápagos Islands because of what the group believed was the inevitability of accidents. BirdLife International had also recommended that cruise ships fuel up outside of the Galápagos Islands because small amounts of fuel spillage are impossible to avoid when transferring fuel between ships.

The *Jessica* incident served as something of a wake-up call for many in the scientific community. Robert Bensted-Smith, director of the Charles Darwin Research Station on the Galápagos, says,

> The image of the *Jessica* spewing fuel into this unique environment has dismayed all who value the natural wonders of the world. Relief that the ecological damage has not, apparently, been severe, must be accompanied by renewed determination to ensure that the archipelago be protected in perpetuity.[34]

Airports

Not every tourist comes to the Galápagos by boat, of course, but the expansion of the airports to meet the increasing tourist influx has generated concern among environmentalists as well as among ornithologists. In the early 1980s two airport expansions allowed for larger-capacity jet aircraft, resulting in increased visitation as well as threats to birds and their habitats.

Every day two commercial jet airliners arrive and depart from the airport on the island of San Cristóbal. Although this is relatively light traffic, environmentalists and ornithologists have reported some bird species vacating nesting areas that lie along the flight paths of the jets. The birds, researchers believe, are moving because of the high noise levels, the vibration, and the smell of jet fuel and exhaust. Ornithologists would prefer that all visitors and residents arrive by boat, but their requests to end air traffic have been denied by Ecuadorian authorities.

In addition to the commercial jets, helicopters are now being used to give tourists a bird's-eye view of the islands

A prehistoric-looking Galápagos land iguana is a sharp contrast to a modern jetliner at an airport on Baltra Island.

and their wildlife. In an effort to provide tourists with unique viewing experiences, private tour companies provide one-hour helicopter rides across several islands and along the beaches. Sometimes flying no more than fifty feet off the ground, the helicopters and the loud slapping sounds of their rotor blades send frightened animals running for cover. Conservationists have objected to the helicopters' negative impact on animals as well as their noise, which annoys ecotourists walking the paths that crisscross the islands. Craig McFarland, former director of the Charles Darwin Foundation, warns about the continuing spread of disruptive activities, including the "unplanned appearance of new tourism activities, such as jet skis, sport harpooning, and helicopter overflights."[35]

Sport fishing

Besides those who come to view the islands' natural wonders are those who come for the excitement of sport fishing. Sport fishermen from around the world have discovered that the deep waters of the Galápagos provide an excellent array of sport fish, such as swordfish, marlins, and dolphins. Prized by anglers for the excitement they provide as they struggle to free themselves from the hook, these large fish are known to fight for several hours before escaping or being brought on board a boat, where they die.

Such sport fishing was once prohibited within forty miles of the islands, but it is now legal in what is called a tag-and-release program. This means that game fish that are caught are tagged with a metal token with the Galápagos logo and are then released. Although the fish are not kept, critics of the tag-and-release program argue that many of the fish pulled on the boats are extremely fragile and are unlikely to survive the trauma of being caught. Furthermore, the fish sometimes swallow the hooks, which cannot be extracted. In such cases, the fishermen can only cut the line and release the fish with the hook imbedded in its stomach. Most fish that suffer this fate will not be able to eat and will slowly die from starvation.

Critics of tag and release also argue that sport fishing is extremely difficult to manage because the GNPS does not have a well-coordinated system to manage the program and no enforcement authority. Without tag-and-release monitors on the sport fishing boats, no one can verify that all fish are released, and few conservationists expect that the guides themselves will enforce the laws.

Species displacement

Even the most considerate and careful visitors to the Galápagos cause problems, however. Tourists who want to experience the wildlife at close quarters often inadvertently invade sensitive habitats, causing animals to withdraw permanently from these areas. This situation is of particular concern to scientists when it involves the habitats of tortoises and other endangered endemic species that have already experienced habitat reduction. As endemic species vacate their habitat to avoid human contact, the delicate balance between animals and their food and breeding habitats can adversely shift.

Tourists move in close to photograph a Galápagos tortoise. Such incidents have led to species displacement as animals try to avoid areas trafficked by tourists.

Rules of the Island

Protecting the habitats and species of the Galápagos is the charter for the Galápagos National Park Service. To this end, the park directors established the following set of rules, which every ecotourist is expected to follow, here quoted by the Charles Darwin Foundation in its website.

1. No plant, animal, or remains of such (including shells, bones, and pieces of wood), or other natural objects should be removed or disturbed.
2. Be careful not to transport any live material to the islands, or from island to island.
3. Do not take any food to the uninhabited islands.
4. Do not touch or handle the animals.
5. Do not feed the animals.
6. Do not startle or chase any animal from its resting or nesting spot.
7. Stay within the areas designated as visiting sites.
8. Do not leave any litter on the islands, or throw any off your boat.
9. Do not deface the rocks.
10. Do not buy souvenirs or objects made of plants or animals from the islands.
11. Do not visit the islands unless accompanied by a licensed National Park guide.
12. Restrict your visits to officially approved areas.
13. Show your conservationist attitude.

In an attempt to avoid flash cameras and the whir of video cameras, animals move away from paths used by tourists. But as these timid animals flee, tourists cut new paths across the landscape as they search for animals to view or photograph. Professor emeritus James Enright of the Scripps Institution of Oceanography in La Jolla, California, has made several visits to the Galápagos and reports that "some of the less populated islands show an increase in the number of tourist trails crisscrossing the unspoiled vegetation."[36] This trend, if not stopped, sets up a chain reaction of still more trails, leading to more animals being displaced.

Craig McFarland, however, is concerned about the future, stating that the current Galápagos ecotourism model developed in Galápagos over the past 30 years has functioned extremely well until now. It has provided for both a high degree of biodiversity and resources protection, as well as for a high quality, and educational visitor experience. However, numerous problems have begun to emerge, which will eventually lead to threats to the system as developed.[37]

The future of ecotourism

Despite the misgivings of conservationists, ecotourism in the Galápagos is increasing and constitutes a threat to the islands' biodiversity and habitats. Just as the fishing industry did in the 1970s, ecotourism will probably continue to expand because of the revenues it generates. According to the International Galapagos Tour Operators Association (IGTOA), tourists generate about $60 million a year, which flows into the economy of the Galápagos; a far greater amount flows into the coffers of the foreign owners of the cruise ships and hotels.

Efforts to attract large sums of tourist money threaten to change the once primitive Galápagos Islands into a tourist mecca. Some observers believe such a change could undermine the efforts of scientists and conservationists. Felipe Cruz, a former park service official who is now a tour guide, knows how much money tour operators can make. Still, he expresses the hope that it is "not too late to prevent the Galápagos from becoming another overdeveloped Hawaii."[38]

Already, conservationists are at odds with tour operators and those in the local community who depend on tourist dollars. According to the IGTOA, plans are already underway for a several-hundred-bed hotel on Isabela, ten times the size of the older and smaller hotels already there. Such large-scale expansion may well end the more gentle form of ecotourism supported by environmentalists during the 1990s.

To some observers, a massive increase in tourism would, by its very nature, destroy what makes the Galápagos unique. Charles Darwin Research Station director Chantal Blanton argues that such large groups are "a bit like being in a theme park. To interact with nature, you just don't do that *en masse*."[39] As one ecotourist guide pointed out facetiously, the best form of ecotourism would be for tourists to send money to the Galápagos for their trip and then not come.

In spite of the problems presented by tourism in its various forms, there is still a chance that the Galápagos will maintain its place as one of the world's great nature preserves. Some people, whose businesses rely on tourism, understand that their economic well-being depends on conserving the environment. These shop, restaurant, and tour company owners recognize that their own economic interests are served by helping conserve the resources that underlie their livelihoods.

5

Conservation

PRESERVING THE GALÁPAGOS Islands for future generations requires addressing the political, ecological, economic, and social needs of the islands without putting further strain on the fragile ecosystem. To achieve these objectives, Galápagos conservation groups are working with Ecuadorian government officials to determine and solve these problems.

During the late 1950s, long before the ecological destruction brought on by the fishing and ecotourism industries, a few farsighted scientists recognized the need to initiate conservation policies to protect endemic species and their habitats. Highest on their list were establishing wildlife reserves, eradicating several of the most destructive invasive species, and establishing breeding programs for endangered Galápagos reptiles. Later, during the late 1990s, the list was lengthened to include restricting ecotourism, inspecting and quarantining, to prevent the introduction of foreign species, and enforcing laws regulating the use of the islands' resources.

Establishing wildlife reserves

The first step that conservationists took to protect and conserve the ecology of the Galápagos was to establish a wildlife reserve. A reserve would place restrictions on habitat use by humans as well as protection for wildlife living there. The objective was to restrict human activity in the reserves to scientific research and restoration, thereby protecting the land and all wildlife from human development and commercial exploitation.

A sign at the Galápagos Islands National Park reminds visitors that the islands' wildlife is protected by law.

In 1959 conservationists working with Ecuadorian government officials established the Galápagos National Park Service (GNPS). This reserve included all islands that had not yet been colonized by Ecuadorian immigrants—97 percent of the total Galápagos landmass. Within this reserve, scientists working with the Ecuadorian government make all policies governing preservation and restoration of habitats. In this area, all wildlife is protected and everyone is forbidden to remove any living species or any part of the habitat.

In 1986 the need to establish a similar reserve for the ocean resulted in the Galápagos Marine Resources Reserve (GMRR), which was established to include all waters within fifteen miles of the Galápagos Islands. Similar to the GNPS, the GMRR radically restricted the use of the coastal waters. For the first time ever, limits were placed on fishing seasons and the numbers of each species that could be caught. The reserve also limited fishing to local residents. With this new piece of legislation in place, conservationists and governmental officials believed they could restore the ecological balance and preserve the endemic species.

Optimism for the GMRR began to wane during the 1990s, as large industrial fishing boats from foreign countries fished the waters right up to the fifteen-mile boundary. Marine biologists quickly realized that foreign high-volume fishing was adversely affecting the coastal fishing within the GMRR. In 1998, to correct this problem, the politicians passed the Galápagos Conservation Law,

 ## New Technologies

Accounting for all of the endangered species on the Galápagos Islands and controlling the spread of tourism has motivated scientists to utilize the latest technologies. The Charles Darwin Research Station (CDRS), in collaboration with the Galápagos National Park Service (GNPS), has worked with many institutions to develop the geographical information system (GIS) to assist scientists in protecting endangered Galápagos species and habitats. In 1999 scientists focused on the need to improve two areas: the development of basic cartography and the incorporation of a global positioning system (GPS).

The CDRS first acquired access to digital maps derived from many maps published in the late 1980s, followed by all Ecuadorian and all U.S. navigational charts through 1995. This collection included a broad array of aerial photography and a series of the most recent satellite imagery.

Many CDRS and GNPS programs are now using the GPS to record ecological monitoring data. These two organizations have also developed new monitoring methods that combine GPS data with sampling techniques to estimate and record the density of various endemic species.

The first sophisticated tests explored patterns of mortality in Galápagos tortoises on Santa Cruz Island. The Isabela Project also used the system to plan a series of monitoring trails on Wolf and Ecuador Volcanoes from satellite imagery, which identified areas of high humidity and dense vegetation. The coordinates of proposed pathways were determined using satellite imagery passed to the GPS by personnel of the Isabela Project. These new trails covered previously unexplored terrain and led to the discovery of some of the densest populations of giant tortoises on the Galápagos.

For the year 2000, emphasis was placed on developing a participatory monitoring program with tourist vessels. In some cases, the vessels carried their own GIS in computers on board that displayed their observations within the context of several environmental variables.

which expanded the protected waters around the archipelago from fifteen to forty miles and limited fishing to Ecuadorians who had been permanently living on the islands for five years or more.

As a result of the Galápagos Conservation Law, the GMRR is now the second-largest marine reserve in the world, after the Great Barrier Reef National Park in Australia. The Marine Reserve Commission oversees the GMRR, and the GNPS is specifically in charge of its protection and management. The reserve now protects some of the best-known coastal fauna of the Galápagos, including sea lions, fur seals, penguins, flightless cormorants, albatrosses, sea turtles, marine iguanas, and several crustaceans and mollusks.

With the establishment of the GNPS, scientists received permission to attack the islands' worst and oldest problem: the invasive species brought to the islands over the previous three centuries.

Eradication of invasive predators

Eradicating the many foreign species that have been introduced to the Galápagos over the past three hundred years continues to be a high priority for conservationists. Experts acknowledge that these animals and plants have caused more destruction of endemic species and habitats than any other factor. Since all of the invasive species still run wild on the islands, survival of the endemic species cannot be guaranteed until the worst of the invaders are eliminated or their numbers are at least controlled.

Heading the list of species to be eradicated are the herds of goats that have severely degraded the habitat of the tortoises—the most threatened species on the islands. The Charles Darwin Research Station (CDRS) and the GNPS estimate a total goat population of 125,000. Of these, 40,000 graze on the island of Isabela, which also has large tortoise populations. Both scientists and government officials have established a major campaign to remove the goats from Isabela as well as from several other islands that have the highest concentrations of tortoises.

Eradicating tens of thousands of goats is a complicated undertaking. A number of strategies were considered for eradicating the goats, but simply shooting them was judged the most humane. In April 1999 hunters were dispatched across several of the islands with high-powered rifles to shoot the goats. Initial projections indicated that it would take between eighteen and twenty-four months, but the goats soon learned to run when they heard the gunshots. After some initial success, hunters realized that the task of removing the goats would take much longer.

As the goat eradication process slowed, innovative ideas were tried to speed up the program. To overcome the problem of goats scattering at the sound of gun shots, officials imported native hunters from the Ecuadorian rain forest who were skilled in the use of silent blowguns and poison darts. This program enjoyed only minimal success, however, so

A sign welcomes visitors to the Charles Darwin Research Station (CDRS). The CDRS is instrumental in attempts to eradicate invasive predators and protect endemic species.

hunters riding in helicopters flew over the islands shooting the goats. This tactic met with some success, but many goats still roamed the islands. Next, trained hunting dogs accompanied the hunters and even satellites were employed to locate herds of goats so that hunters could plan the best way to surprise and kill as many animals as possible.

The goat populations have been dramatically reduced but not eliminated. The same is true of the pig population,

A New Threat: Galápagos Farmers

As scientists and conservationists labor to cure the old ills of the islands, Galápagos farmers are busily introducing new ones. Far from the fishermen and tourists who wreak their own forms of environmental destruction, farmers are unwittingly introducing new ones as they develop farmland for the first time ever.

Many problems are caused by introducing farms. The importation of cattle to the islands means a loss of habitat for endemic species as well as a threat to the natural habitat. Although cows are not as destructive as goats, they nonetheless dominate large pastures and trample threatened vegetation as well as nesting areas for birds and reptiles.

Introducing cattle also creates a series of problems never before encountered. As cows enter the islands, they carry with them destructive insects. Many insect species live on cattle and easily find their way onto the islands without being detected. Cows also introduce unusually large volumes of waste in the form of urine and manure, which are washed down to the coastline with the rains. Environmentalists do not yet know the potential extent of dangers introduced by cattle.

Foreign crops such as corn, tomatoes, and vegetables are an additional issue. As these hearty crops turn profits for farmers, conservationists fear their acreage will spread into territory currently reserved for endemic species. The conflict between conservationists and local farmers is heating up, and some fear that local economics may eclipse concern for the well-being of endemic species and habitats.

although their numbers have been reduced to an estimated fifteen hundred animals. As a result, the reduced pig population no longer poses a serious threat to the tortoises.

The scourge of feral dogs and rats is also being addressed. These two intruders are being eradicated by poison. Biscuits made of poison but with the smell and taste of food have been scattered about the islands. These biscuits are safe to use because they do not resemble the foods eaten by birds or reptiles. Biologists place biscuits down holes where rats and dogs search for eggs and hatchlings. So far, the biscuits have markedly reduced the rat and dog populations.

Controlling the invasive species allows biologists to focus on increasing the endangered endemic species. Hoping to avoid the extinction of any more Galápagos species, scientists are putting measures in place to increase the populations of those that are the most threatened.

Breeding programs for endangered species

The third piece of the conservation program is to increase the numbers of endangered species. The species most in need of assistance is the Galápagos tortoise. On the island of Española, for example, only fourteen tortoises remained in 1963. Competition with goats was so intense that a scientist walking this island reported seeing a single tortoise eating a cactus pad surrounded by fifteen goats doing the same thing. On Pinta Island, only one surviving member of a subspecies of Galápagos tortoise can be found. The death of this animal, named Lonesome George, will signal another extinction. Because a few of the tortoise habitats continue to be overrun by predators, scientists made the decision to raise newly hatched tortoises in the safety of man-made enclosures. The staff at the CDRS and their colleagues in the GNPS began the tortoise-breeding program in 1965. The program begins with biologists, who locate and monitor females in the wild and wait for them to lay their eggs. After the females deposit their eggs, biologists dig them up and place them in incubators, where they are safe from pigs and dogs. When the

Lonesome George

The sole remaining tortoise of one subspecies, *geochelone elephanto-phus abingdoni*, was named Lonesome George by herpetologists who found him roaming Pinta Island in 1970. Surprised to discover this rare subspecies, herpetologists scoured the island hoping to find a female, but they had no luck.

Instead, herpetologists decided to try to mate him with a female of a different subspecies, even though any offspring would create another subspecies. The herpetologists immediately began a breeding program using two females, but over the next decade neither laid fertile eggs.

Just why George, believed by herpetologists to be between fifty and eighty years old, was either disinterested in or incapable of mating remains a mystery. On February 5, 2001, reporter Simon Gardner, working for the Reuters news agency, interviewed herpetologist Solanda Rea of the Charles Darwin Research Station on Santa Cruz Island, who has been breeding tortoises to boost dwindling numbers for nearly twenty years. Rea said in this interview, which appears in an article titled "Lonesome George Faces Own Galapagos Tortoise Curse," "We don't really know what the problem is, he just runs out of steam when trying to copulate. In theory he should be able to mate with the two females we have put with him, but I think that after so many years living alone, he just needs a female of his own sub-species."

Cloning was at one time considered, but scientists have now ruled it out. At this time, George's subspecies will become extinct upon his death. That, however, may not occur for another 150 years.

Lonesome George is the last known living specimen of his subspecies.

A naturalist at the CDRS feeds a giant tortoise. The CDRS has been involved in a successful breeding program since 1965 that had reintroduced twenty-five hundred young tortoises to the islands by the year 2000.

eggs hatch, the babies are moved into pens, where they are fed, observed, painted with an identifying number on their carapaces, and protected. The tortoises are reared in corrals covered by anti-rat screens, where they remain for five years. At that time, their carapaces are measured, and if they have reached eight inches, biologists consider them large enough to be reintroduced into their natural habitat with minimal threat from other species.

This breeding program has been highly successful. In the year 2000, thirty-five years after this program began, it had reintroduced twenty-five hundred young tortoises, most of which have survived. The identifying number on each tortoise's carapace allows herpetologists to monitor them in the wild to assess their development and their impact on the habitat.

Botanists, just like zoologists, have breeding programs aimed at reintroducing endemic plant species back into the native habitat. Botanists are undertaking a program never before attempted in the Galápagos: the restoration of an endemic plant threatened by extinction. Since 1999, botanist Vanessa Coronel has been leading the study of the threatened opuntia plant of Española Island, with the hope of reestablishing its population.

The opuntia is listed as an endangered species because of goats that eat it and because of decreases in the giant tortoise, which disperses opuntia seeds by eating them and later depositing them in their excrement. Prior to the program to breed this species, its survival was in doubt because of restricted distribution and poor regeneration. Today, however, Coronel is reestablishing the opuntia population by using seedlings grown in a laboratory in addition to samples collected on other islands.

As a result of this program, eight- to ten-month-old opuntia seedlings have been planted on Española Island to reestablish the plant population. Survival rates of these seedlings have jumped from an initial 21 percent to a current 70 percent.

Restricting ecotourism

In 1998, to further protect endangered plants and animals, the Ecuadorian government created a new set of laws for the Galápagos aimed at placing greater control over ecotourism. Conservationists studying the impact of ecotourists on the Galápagos habitats saw evidence of destruction and recommended laws restricting ecotourism to protect the environment.

The new laws focus on restricting ecotourism in order to protect the biodiversity of the islands and to prevent further habitat destruction and the introduction of any further foreign species. Numerous provisions lessen the impact of ecotourists as they walk the islands and explore the underwater marine species along the fragile coastline.

The key component of the laws addresses the problem of tourist density and limits the number of tourists to sixty thousand a year. Further restrictions mandate which islands may be visited and where on those islands tourists

may go. The more sensitive areas are off limits to tourists altogether, but enough different areas are open to tourists so that even places that tourists visit will not be overrun.

To lessen the impact of tourists on the islands, the CDRS recommended the establishment of three tourist zones, which the Ecuadorian government implemented. These zones designate extensive use, intensive use, and recreational use. Eleven extensive-use zones now exist, scattered across seven islands. In these zones, group sizes are limited to sixteen visitors, and only one group at a time may visit a particular zone. Twenty-one intensive-use zones are distributed over fifteen islands and are for use by multiple groups at a time. Nineteen recreational-use zones on the four inhabited islands are set aside for use by local residents and by visitors seeking recreation, education, hiking, and camping.

The new laws also mandate that tourists may no longer walk the islands alone; they now must be accompanied by a licensed guide. These guides must attend classes, following which they receive a license. While leading groups of

A Galápagos land iguana feeds on an opuntia cactus. Efforts are underway to prevent the extinction of this endemic plant on Española Island.

tourists, guides must monitor all tourist activities to ensure that none of the habitat is disturbed. The law also establishes a ratio of tourists to guides that cannot exceed sixteen tourists for each guide, which means that all tourists are closely monitored.

The tourist zones also apply to the marine environment. Tourists who wish to scuba dive or fish the waters of the marine preserve must do so from boats licensed by the government. The operators of these boats must demonstrate a knowledge of the laws regulating the use of the marine preserve and must prevent tourists from harming or removing any species. Boat operators are held responsible for ensuring that all fish that are caught are quickly released.

Inspection and quarantine

A tourist explores the islands accompanied by a local guide. Laws now require visitors to be accompanied by licensed guides when they tour the islands.

Preventing any further invasions of foreign species is an ongoing objective of Galápagos scientists. The preventive component is complex because each person, whether a resident or tourist, directly or indirectly, uses cargo boats, airplanes, and land vehicles, which are also the means of transport for introduced organisms. Preventing the en-

trance of invasive species is far more efficient than treating the problems caused by invasive species after they take hold on the islands.

In May 1999 the CDRS collaborated with other institutions, including the GNPS and agricultural departments, to establish the System of Inspection and Quarantine for Galápagos (SIQGAL). This system attempts to prevent the introduction of foreign species to the islands, to permit the search of boats and airplanes for any species, and to assure that imported products are in good, sanitary condition. As of 2002, any person who wishes to enter the Galápagos or to transport cargo must observe a list of permitted products and obey strict sanitary regulations.

As a result of recent inspections, SIQGAL personnel have intercepted a number of plants, animals, and injurious pests. Among them are a species of grass known to be an aggressive weed, an insect that is currently destroying endemic plants on the coast of mainland Ecuador, mangoes carrying the larvae of a destructive fruit fly, and larger foreign species of animals such as crabs, mollusks, and even a rabbit.

Ecuador has also imposed a quarantine system to reduce the flow of invasive pests. Large animals of commercial value, such as horses and cattle, must be quarantined at their port of entry until veterinarians are able to inspect them for diseases that might spread to other Galápagos animals. In addition, the animals are checked for any insects they might be carrying. Until animals are cleared by veterinarians, they may not proceed to their destinations.

SIQGAL personnel have managed to detect and prevent the entry of a number of would-be invaders. However, as the numbers of Ecuadorians and tourists increase, each year the task gets harder. Craig McFarland, president of the foundation that runs the CDRS, says the long-term solution to controlling invasive species is

> to find a way to stem the island's population explosion which right now is running at 8 percent a year. The frightening thing about the last 15 to 20 years is that as this huge population increase has occurred, the rate of introduction of these foreign species has gone up—has gone up very sharply.[40]

Law enforcement

The GMRR, which was officially created as a protected area, was failing to achieve its objective of safeguarding endangered marine species because Ecuadorian police officers were reluctant to punish violators of the fishing regulations. The large foreign fleets were illegally taking pelagic fish within the established forty-mile reserve, and the local fishing community was exceeding established limits for coastal lobsters and sea cucumbers. In spite of these violations, none of the offenders was arrested or fined.

Although the GMRR has authority to recommend the arrest of fishing violators, only the Ecuadorian government has the authority to arrest, prosecute, and punish violators. During the GMRR's first few years, government police only issued warnings to offenders. Because of this lenient policy, some fishermen continued to illegally catch fish and marine invertebrates within the forty-mile reserve.

In 1995, however, the GMRR requested that the government purchase a patrol boat that would enable its crew to board and inspect fishing boats and, if necessary, arrest the crew and impound their boats. For the first time, boat owners recognized that they might be punished for illegal fishing. According to news reporter Richard Harris, speaking in 1995, the fines were finally being levied: "Two large tuna boats from the mainland are anchored in the harbor this day. They've been brought in to pay a fine for illegal fishing in the marine reserve that surrounds the islands."[41]

A separate incident in 1997 cost a Japanese boat captain his entire catch and five days in jail. The boat was boarded within the forty-mile reserve, and fish were found in the hold. The captain argued that the fish had been caught beyond the forty-mile boundary and that he was headed to the Galápagos for needed engine repairs. The police, however, did not believe him and confiscated his entire catch and held him and his ship for five days.

Sometimes a violation can cost a boat owner dearly. On December 10, 1999, seventeen hundred pounds of sea cucumbers were seized from a boat headed for a dock in

Ecuador. The harbor master there, alerted by a staff member of the GNPS, boarded the boat and discovered the sea cucumbers, a box of shark fins, and lobsters that were below the permitted minimum size. The entire shipment was taken from the boat owners and their boat was seized.

Conservationists working with the Ecuadorian government hope the recent "get tough" policy on the part of the police will stop illegal fishing. Although many fishermen understand the importance of protecting the dwindling fishing stocks, others will only stop if they know that they will be arrested and punished.

Tourists are also subject to arrest if rules are violated. To enforce the laws governing tourism, penalties ranging from fines to imprisonment are prescribed for tourists who violate any of the laws governing their activities. Of greatest concern is harm to wildlife and habitat. Andy Drumm, director of the Nature Conservancy's ecotourism program,

Tourists board a boat on the shore of Bartolome Island in the Galápagos. Violating laws governing their activities can result in tourists being fined or imprisoned.

comments, "These new standards will help ensure that tourists and the revenue they generate are helping to protect these great yet fragile places."[42]

To give endemic species and their habitats breathing space, humans must find ways to reduce their impact on the Galápagos. This means stabilizing and ultimately reducing the human population while continuing to reduce the populations of invasive species. For those people who must live on the islands, it also means increasing efficiency in the use of materials and energy as well as intelligently planning and managing community infrastructure. Additionally, it means establishing educational standards that build an awareness of responsibility in managing the results of hundreds of thousands of years' worth of biological evolution.

Preventing the loss of the Galápagos wildlife can be accomplished if the current steps to protect and preserve endemic species are continued. These steps, of course, must be balanced against the needs of the human habitants of the islands.

Some conservationists would like to see all humans forever removed from the islands, but local politicians want to see the revenue from continued ecotourism used to pay for community improvements such as piped water, sewers, medical clinics, and schools. Both conservationists and islanders might benefit from sustainable development if all parties are involved in the tricky process of balancing both ecological conservation and development. The Galápagos, after all, can neither be returned to the time before its discovery in 1535, nor can it be sealed off from the public forever. It remains to be seen whether reckless ecotourism and development will be allowed to devalue the Galápagos into yet another theme park or whether this unique natural habitat can be preserved for the enjoyment and wonder of generations to come.

Notes

Introduction

1. Quoted in Galapagos.com, www.galapagos.com/
animal.htm#reptiles.

2. Quoted in Harry Thurston, "Last Look at Paradise? The
Primordial World of the Galapagos Is Under Siege from People,"
International Wildlife, May 15, 1997, p. 12.

Chapter 1: A Place Like Nowhere Else

3. Charles Darwin, *The Voyage of the "Beagle."* New
York: Prometheus Books, 2000, p. 400.

4. Darwin, *The Voyage of the "Beagle,"* p. 398.

5. Darwin, *The Voyage of the "Beagle,"* p. 405.

6. Darwin, *The Voyage of the "Beagle,"* p. 411.

7. Darwin, *The Voyage of the "Beagle,"* pp. 408–409.

8. Darwin, *The Voyage of the "Beagle,"* p. 417.

9. Darwin, *The Voyage of the "Beagle,"* pp. 415–16.

Chapter 2: Invasive Species

10. Quoted in TerraQuest, "History of Galápagos—First
Explorers." www.terraquest.com/galapagos/index.html.

11. Darwin, *The Voyage of the "Beagle,"* p. 399.

12. Quoted in Environmental News Network, "Study
Documents New Threats to Galápagos Islands." www.enn.
com/enn-news-archive/1997/07/071897/07189711.asp.

13. Quoted in *Scientific American Frontiers,* "Ask the
Scientists: Martin Wikelski." www.pbs.org/safarchive/3_ask/
archive/qna/32101_wikelski.html.

14. Charles Darwin Foundation, "The Isabela Project:

Ambitious Work of Ecological Restoration." www.darwinfoundation.org/Ourwork/terrest/t9.html.

15. Quoted in Charles Darwin Foundation, "Latitudinal Temperature Variations," *Galápagos Conservation Trust Newsletter*, Autumn 1995, p. 16.

16. Quoted in Alden M. Hayashi, "Attack of the Fire Ants," *Scientific American*, February 1, 1999, p. 26.

17. Quoted in Richard Harris, "Galapagos Islands at the Crossroads," part 2, *All Things Considered,* National Public Radio, December 19, 1995.

18. Quoted in Harris, "Galapagos Islands at the Crossroads," part 2.

Chapter 3: Fishing Threats

19. Monte Hayes, "Humans Biggest Threat to Galapagos," *Associated Press*, January 28, 2001. http://wire.ap.org/APNews/?SITE=KYELI&FRONTID=HOME.

20. Rodrigo Bustamante, *Biodiversity Conservation in the Galápagos Marine Reserve.* Washington, DC: Charles Darwin Foundation, 1998, p.7.

21. Roger Payne, "Voyage of the *Odyssey:* the Galápagos," Public Broadcasting System. www.pbs.org/odyssey/odyssey/galapagos_logs.html.

22. Andrea Dorfman, "Environment: On the Brink Highlights from the New Red List of Species Headed for Extinction," *Time,* October 9, 2000, p. 92.

23. Pippa Heylings, *Summary of the Changes and Advances in the Management and Protection of the Galápagos Marine Reserve*. Washington, DC: Charles Darwin Foundation, June 1999, p. 2.

24. Pelagic Shark Rescue Foundation, "Conservation." www.pelagic.org/conservation.

25. Jerry T. Goldsmith, interview by author, San Diego, California, May 18, 2001.

26. Quoted in Environmental News Network, "Sea Cucumber

Protection Failing." www.enn.com/enn-news-archive/1999/03/030299/cucumber_1881.asp.

27. Quoted in TerraQuest, "Virtual Galápagos." www.terraquest.com/galapagos/index.html.

28. Quoted in Thurston, "Last Look at Paradise?" p. 17.

Chapter 4: Ecotourism Threats

29. Craig McFarland, *An Analysis of Nature Tourism in the Galápagos Islands*. Washington, DC: Charles Darwin Foundation, 2000, p. 146.

30. Quoted in Environmental News Network, "Swamped by Eco-Tourists, Island Park Directors Set Limits," March 12, 2001. www.enn.com/enn-news-archive/2001/03/03122001/ecotourism_42457.asp.

31. Quoted in TerraQuest, "Virtual Galápagos."

32. Environmental News Network, "Smog Spreads in Remote Tropical Paradises." www.enn.com/enn-news-archive/1998/04/040298/smog_21471.asp.

33. Martha Honey, "Paying the Price of Ecotourism; Two Pioneer Biological Reserves Face the Challenges Brought by a Recent Boom in Tourism. (Ecuador's Galapagos Islands and Costa Rica's Monteverde Cloud Forest Reserve)," *Americas,* November 1, 1994, p. 43.

34. Robert Bensted-Smith, World Wildlife Fund, www.worldwildlife.org/galapagos.

35. McFarland, *An Analysis of Nature Tourism in the Galápagos Islands*, p. 167.

36. James Enright, interview by author, La Jolla, California, May 16, 2001.

37. McFarland, *An Analysis of Nature Tourism in the Galápagos Islands,* p. 161.

38. Quoted in Harris, "Galapagos Islands at the Crossroads," part 2.

39. Quoted in Honey, "Paying the Price of Ecotourism; Two Pioneer Biological Reserves Face the Challenges

Brought by a Recent Boom in Tourism," p. 49.

Chapter 5: Conservation

40. Quoted in Harris, "Galapagos Islands at the Crossroads," part 2.

41. Richard Harris, "Galapagos Islands at the Crossroads," part 1, *All Things Considered,* National Public Radio, December 18, 1995.

42. Environmental News Network, "Swamped by Eco-Tourists, Island Park Directors Set Limits."

Organizations
to Contact

Charles Darwin Foundation for the Galápagos Islands
407 N. Washington St.
Suite 105
Falls Church, VA 22046
(703) 538-6833
e-mail: Darwin@galapagos.org
www.darwinfoundation.org
The Charles Darwin Foundation exists to provide knowledge
and support to ensure the conservation of the environment
and biodiversity of the Galápagos archipelago through scientific research and complementary actions.

Environmental News Network (ENN)
2020 Milvia
Suite 411
Berkeley, CA 94704
(510) 644-3661
fax: (208) 475-7986
e-mail: mgt@enn.com
www.enn.com/index.asp
The Environmental News Network has been working to edu-
cate the world about environmental issues facing the earth.

The Galápagos Coalition
Dept. of Geology
Sonoma State University
1801 E. Cotati Ave.
Rohnert Park, CA 94928
(707) 664-2301

fax: (707) 664-2505

http://serv1.law.emory.edu/sites/GALAPAGOS

The Galápagos Coalition website focuses on research, environmental alerts and laws governing preservation of Galápagos species, in addition to a good collection of maps and video tapes.

The Pelagic Shark Rescue Foundation

100 Shaffer Rd.

Santa Cruz, CA 95060

(408) 459-9346

e-mail: psrf@pelagic.org

www.pelagic.org/conservation

The mission of PSRF is to develop and assist projects that contribute to a better understanding of sharks, with an emphasis on those which contribute to their conservation and management.

Recfishwest

PO Box 57

Claremont

Western Australia

Australia 6010

http://recfishwest.org.au

The mission of Recfishwest is to maintain recreational fishing as a rewarding experience and to be an effective voice in all forums to promote the interests of all recreational fishers.

TRAFFIC

219c Huntingdon Rd.

Cambridge CB3 0DL, United Kingdom

+44 (0) 1223 277427

fax: +44 (0) 1223 277237

e-mail: traffic@trafficint.org

www.traffic.org

TRAFFIC's mission is to ensure that trade in wild plants and animals is not a threat to the conservation of nature. This website posts the illegal sale and trade of endangered species of all types and discusses conservation measures needed to ensure the survival of the most endangered animals around the world.

World Wildlife Fund
1250 24th WWF
Suite 500
Washington, DC 20037
(202) 293-4800
www.worldwildlife.org/galapagos
World Wildlife Fund is dedicated to protecting the world's wildlife and wildlands and is the largest privately supported international conservation organization in the world. Since its inception in 1961, WWF has invested in over 13,100 projects in 157 countries.

Suggestions for Further Reading

Books

Craig McFarland, *An Analysis of Nature Tourism in the Galá-pagos Islands*. Washington, DC: Charles Darwin Foundation, 2000. This work is a detailed analysis and list of recommen-dations for the preservation and control of ecotourism on the Galápagos.

Craig McFarland and M. Cifuentes, *Case Study: Galapa-gos, Ecuador*. Washington, DC: Charles Darwin Founda-tion, 1996. This work is a detailed discussion of the present status of human intervention on the Galápagos by Ecuado-rian residents as well as tourists. The report discusses the impact of humans on the local flora and fauna.

I. Thorton, *Darwin's Islands: A Natural History of the Galapa-gos*. New York: Natural History, 1971. This book provides a good discussion of the history of the Galápagos from Darwin's visit until the early 1970s. Because of the publication date, the book does not touch on the ecotourism issue.

Periodicals

M. Camhi, "Industrial Fisheries Threaten Ecological Integrity of Galapagos," *Biological Conservation*, vol. 28, 1995.

R. S. de Groot, "Tourism and Conservation in the Galapagos Islands," *Biological Conservation,* vol. 26, 1983.

S. Itow, "Altitudinal Change in Plant Endemism, Species Turnover, and Diversity on Isla Santa Cruz, the Galapagos Is-lands," *Pacific Science,* vol. 46, 1992.

M. D. Lemonick, "Can the Galapagos Survive?" *Time,* November 6, 1995.

New Scientist, "Wildlife on Galapagos Still in Danger," June 1985.

F. Pearce, "Galapagos Tortoises Under Siege," *New Scientist,* September 1995.

Scientific American, "Evolution's Workshop Considers the Parade of Sailors, Scientists, Poachers and Eccentrics Who Have Visited the Galapagos Islands," February 2001.

Websites

Charles Darwin Foundation for the Galápagos Islands (www.darwinfoundation.org/). This website is dedicated to continuing the work begun by Charles Darwin and to promoting the conservation of rare and endangered flora and fauna on the Galápagos Islands. This website provides a comprehensive database dealing with all issues relevant to the islands as well as ongoing research.

Environmental News Network (www.enn.com). This website presents a wide array of current news that relates to environmental issues. Coverage includes national and international politics, business and the economy, environmental legislation, and stories about environmental threats.

Galápagos Coalition (http://serv1.law.emory.edu/sites/GALAPAGOS/). The Galápagos Coalition website focuses on research, environmental alerts, laws governing preservation of native species, and has a good collection of maps and videos.

Pelagic Shark Rescue Foundation (www.pelagic.org/conservation/). This website provides a detailed database for the study of all species of sharks, information about the role of sharks in the environment, how they are commercially used, and threats to their survival.

Reuters (http://reuters.com/). Reuters news agency provides a website of current national and international news. Updated daily, it provides an excellent source for leading news stories.

TerraQuest (www.terraquest.com/galapagos/). This website provides a vast assortment of articles pertaining to the Galápagos Islands. Its focus is on conservation, current issues on biodiversity, and discussions on the history and future of the Galápagos. The maps are excellent.

TRAFFIC (www.traffic.org/). TRAFFIC's mission is to ensure that trade in wild plants and animals is not a threat to the conservation of nature. This website posts the illegal sale and trade of endangered species of all types and discusses conservation measures needed to ensure the survival of the most endangered animals around the world.

World Wildlife Fund (www.worldwildlife.org/galapagos). This website provides current information on potential environmental threats to the Galápagos Islands as well as information about the islands' plants and animals.

Works Consulted

Books

Rodrigo Bustamante, *Biodiversity Conservation in the Galápagos Marine Reserve*. Washington, DC: Charles Darwin Foundation, 1998. A technical study focused on the impact of mechanized fishing techniques in the Galápagos waters.

Charles Darwin, *The Voyage of the "Beagle."* New York: Prometheus Books, 2000. Charles Darwin's journal of his travels and discoveries while on board the British ship the *Beagle*. It details his travels and discoveries. Chapter 17 describes his five-week stay on the Galápagos Islands.

Pippa Heylings, *Summary of the Changes and Advances in the Management and Protection of the Galápagos Marine Reserve.* Washington, DC: Charles Darwin Foundation, June 1999. This publication studies problems in the Galápagos ecosystem and makes recommendations for improving the management of the marine environment.

Martha Honey, *Ecotourism and Sustainable Development: Who Owns Paradise?* Washington, DC: Island, 1999. The author presents an overview of the ecotourism industry and a firsthand account of ecotourism projects around the world. Honey offers a vivid description and analysis of projects that meet the goals and standards of ecotourism as well as those that claim to be ecotourism but are not. In-depth case studies of seven destinations include the Galápagos, Costa Rica, Cuba, Zanzibar, Tanzania, Kenya, and South Africa.

Richard Lee Marks, *Three Men of the "Beagle."* New York: Alfred A. Knopf, 1991. Although this is a fictional book, it accurately tells the story of the voyage of the *Beagle*. The book recounts Darwin's experiences on the ship, the significance of the trip in terms of his scientific contributions, and Darwin's relationship with the ship's captain and with Jemmy Button, a native of Tierra del Fuego. This book highlights the events leading to Darwin's writings about natural selection and evolution.

Periodicals

Andrea Dorfman, "Environment: On the Brink Highlights from the New Red List of Species Headed for Extinction," *Time,* October 9, 2000.

Alden M. Hayashi, "Attack of the Fire Ants," *Scientific American,* February 1, 1999.

Martha Honey, "Paying the Price of Ecotourism; Two Pioneer Biological Reserves Face the Challenges Brought by a Recent Boom in Tourism. (Ecuador's Galapagos Islands and Costa Rica's Monteverde Cloud Forest Reserve)," *Americas,* November 1, 1994.

Harry Thurston, "Last Look at Paradise? The Primordial World of the Galapagos Is Under Siege from People," *International Wildlife,* May 15, 1997.

Internet Sources

Charles Darwin Foundation, "The Isabela Project: Ambitious Work of Ecological Restoration." www.darwinfoundation. org/Ourwork/terrest/t9.html.

Environmental News Network, "Sea Cucumber Protection Failing." www.enn.com/enn-news-archive/1999/03/030299/cucumber_1881.asp.

———, "Smog Spreads in Remote Tropical Paradises." www.enn.com/enn-news-archive/1998/04/040298/smog_21471. asp.

———, "Study Documents New Threats to Galapagos Islands." www.enn.com/enn-news-archive/1997/07/0701897/070189711.asp.

———, "Swamped by Eco-Tourists, Island Park Directors Set Limits," March 12, 2001. www.enn.com/enn-news-archive/2001/03/03122001/ecotourism_42457.asp.

Galapagos.com. www.galapagos.com/animal.htm#reptiles.

Monte Hayes, "Humans Biggest Threat to Galapagos," Associated Press, January 28, 2001. http://wire.ap.org/APNews/?SITE=KYELI&FRONTID=HOME.

Roger Payne, "Voyage of the *Odyssey*: The Galápagos," Public Broadcasting System. www.pbs.org/odyssey/odysseygalapagos_logs.html.

Pelagic Shark Rescue Foundation, "Conservation." www.pelagic.org/conservation.

Scientific American Frontiers, "Ask the Scientists: Martin Wikelski." www.pbs.org/safarchive/3_ask/archive/qna/32101_wikelski.html.

TerraQuest, "History of Galápagos—First Explorers." www.terraquest.com/galapagos/index.html.

———, "Virtual Galápagos." www.terraquest.com/galapagos/index.html.

Radio Program

Richard Harris, "Galapagos Islands at the Crossroads." Parts 1 and 2. *All Things Considered*, National Public Radio, December 18, 1995.

Index

animals. *see* endemic species;
 invasive species
Antarctica, 25
Asia
 sea cucumbers and, 56–57
 sharks and, 49
Association of Park Wardens of
 the Galápagos National Park
 Service, 59
Australia, 28
Azores, 12

Barry, Jonathan, 9
Baquerizo Moreno (port), 69
Bejarano, Gustavo Noboa, 59
Bensted-Smith, Robert
 on the *Jessica,* 70
Berlanga, Tomás de, 31
biodiversity, 11–12
 coastal region and, 22
 isolation and, 13
 of marine region, 27
BirdLife International, 70
Blanton, Chantal
 on ecotourism, 75–76
 on human greed and problems,
 60
Brown, David
 on solid waste and wildlife, 65
Bustamante, Rodrigo
 on industrial fishing, 48

Cambridge University, 14
Charles Darwin Foundation
 (CDF), 9, 61, 72
 as educational facility, 63
 island rules on website of,
 74
 need for ecotourism, 63
 report on feral rats by, 37
Charles Darwin Research Station
 (CDRS), 42, 70, 75
 eradication of goats and, 80
 new technologies used by, 79
 program to eliminate invasive
 plants by, 34
 violence against, 59–60
climate
 El Niño and, 55
 microclimates, 23
 ocean currents and, 14–15,
 24–25
 wind and, 30
coastal region
 importance of scavengers in, 22
 microclimates and, 23
 sandy shores and, 24
 sewage and, 66–67
conservation
 breeding endangered species
 and, 83–86
 eradication of invasive predators and, 80–83

inspection and quarantine and,
88–89
law enforcement and, 90–92
restriction of ecotourism and,
86–88
wildlife reserves and, 77–80
Coronel, Vanessa
study of opuntia plant, 86
Cousteau, Jacques, 6

Darwin, Charles, 14
on biodiversity, 13
visit by, 27–29
Deal, Michael, 26–27
on food chain of deep sea fish,
26–27
Devonport (England), 28
Dorfman, Andrea
on long-line fishing, 53
Drumm, Andy
on ecotourism laws, 91–92
on unregulated tourism, 64, 74

ecosystems
balance of, 10–11
threatened, 6–7
Ecuador, 6, 35
air traffic and, 71–72
conservation and, 77
enforcement of Galápagos laws
and, 59
fishing and, 57
immigrants from, 58
laws on ecotourism and, 86
Ecuador Volcano, 79
endemic species, 6, 10
biodiversity of, 11–13
birds, 30

of coastal region, 22
effect of aircraft on, 71–72
miconia, 9
opuntia plant, 86
penguins, 37
England, 14
Enright, James
on tourists, 74
environment
damage by ships' anchors to, 8
human pollution and, 58–61
maritime disaster and, 68–70
pollution and, 9
resorts and, 62
tourism and, 64–67
Environmental News Network
on smog, 66
Española Island, 83, 86

farmers, 44–45, 82
fishing, 8–9, 45–46, 59–60
coastal, 56–58
collateral damage by, 52–56
enforcement of laws and, 90
high-tech, 50–52
limits on season and catch,
78–79
pelagic, 47–50
restrictions on, 56–57
tag-and-release program and,
72–73
Fitzroy (captain), 26
French Academy of Sciences, 14

Galápagos Coalition, 65
Galápagos Conservation Law,
79, 80
Galápagos Explorer (cruise

ship) 69–70

Galápagos iguanas
  exotic predators and, 35–36
  land, 19–20
  marine, 20–22

Galápagos Islands
  discovery of, 27
  climates of, 14–16
  ecodiversity of, 6
  exotic predators and, 35
  geography of, 13–16
  geologic origins of, 6, 15–16,
    43
  human population and, 7,
    46–47, 58–61
  isolation and, 27–29
  lack of docking facilities in, 68
  microclimates and, 16
  natural history of, 29–30
  Park Service rules on, 74
  pirates and, 32
  predators and, 34–40
  social conflict over, 59
  whalers and, 32–33
  see also coastal region; marine
    region

Galápagos Marine Resources
  Reserve (GMRR), 78, 80

Galápagos National Park Service
  (GNPS), 8–9, 34, 42
  established by Ecuador, 78
  fishing and deaths of large
    marine birds, 53
  funding and ecotourism and,
    63–64
  new technologies and, 79

Galápagos tortoise, 16, 19
  breeding of, 83–85

egg mortality, 37
  exotic predators and, 35–36
  garbage as threat to, 65
  gender determination of, 39
  human contact and, 73–75
  Lonesome George, 84
  miconia plant and, 43
  microclimates and, 17
  Spanish name of, 31
  survival techniques of, 18

Gardner, Simon, 84

Gibbs, James P., 41–42

goats, 33, 40
  attempts to eradicate, 80–83
  destruction of flora by, 38–39
  habitat degradations by, 37–38

Goldsmith, Jerry T.
  on sharks as scavengers, 54

GPS (Global Positioning
  System), 79

Great Barrier Reef National Park
  (Australia), 80

Harris, Richard
  on enforcement of fishing laws,
    90

Hayes, Monte
  on fishing, 47

Heylings, Pippa
  on drowning of important
    species, 53

HMS Beagle (ship), 14, 28

Honey, Martha
  on ecotourism, 68

human population, 7, 31
  migration of, 9
  pirates, 32
  poaching and, 55

pollution and, 9, 58–61, 66
resorts and, 62
restrictions on habitat use by,
   77
stabilizing and reducing, 92
Humboldt Current, 23

insects
  fire ants, 41–42
  importance to food chain, 40
International Galápagos Tour
  Operators Association
  (IGTOA), 75
invasive species, 31–32, 36,
  38–41
  cats, 35, 37
  cattle, 35
  cinchona tree, 42
  combating, 34
  dogs, 7, 33, 37, 83
  guava and mango, 44–45
  herbicides and, 43
  horse, 25
  inspection and quarantine for,
    88–89
  pigs, 33, 37
  rats, 7, 33, 37, 83
Isabela Island, 42, 80
  dog attacks on, 36
Isabela Project, 79

Jessica (fuel tanker), 69–70

Larson, Tom
  on cinchona tree, 43–44

marine region
  biodiversity of, 27

deepwater fish and, 24
marine currents and, 24–26,
  29–30
Marine Reserve Commission, 80
Marine Reserve of Galápagos,
  59
McFarland, Craig
  on controlling invasive species,
    89
  on future of ecotourism, 75
  on helicopter overflights, 72
  on tourism, 61
Muliken, Teresa
  on sea cucumber extraction, 57

Nature Conservancy, 64, 91
New York State University, 42
New Zealand, 28

Overview of World Trade in
  Sharks and Other
  Cartilaginous Fishes, An
  (TRAFFIC), 49

Panama, 31
Patagonia, 28
Pawson, David
  on sea cucumber, 57
Payne, Roger
  on declining fish populations,
    52
Pelagic Shark Rescue
  Foundation
  on by-catch deaths, 53–54
Pellerano, Miguel
  on predators threat to endemic
    species, 25
Pinta Island, 83

Pinzón Island, 37
Province of Galápagos, 59

Rea, Solanda, 84
  on breeding program, 94
Rodriguez, Evan
  on miconia plant, 43
Royal Society, 14

San Cristóbal Island, 69, 71
Santa Cruz Island, 60, 79, 84
  garbage dump on, 75–76
  wild dogs on, 26
Scripps Institution of
  Oceanography, 74
sea cucumbers, 56–58
sea lions
  birthing places of, 24
  garbage as threat to, 65
  sharks and, 50
seals
  birthing of, 24
  sharks and, 50
Sea World (San Diego), 54
sharks, 47
  importance of, 54
  shortage of, 48–50
System of Inspection and
  Quarantine for Galápagos
  (SIQGAL), 89

Tahiti, 28
Terrestrial National Park, 59
theories

of evolution, 14
of natural selection, 14
Tierra del Fuego, 28
tourism, 8–9, 62–63, 76–77
  activities and, 72
  airports and, 70–72
  conservationists and, 75
  cruise ships and, 61, 67–70
  laws and, 91
  lights from resorts, 54–55
  pollution and, 64–67
  species displacement and,
    73–75
  sport fishing and, 72–73
  tourist zones, 87–88
TRAFFIC, 57
  and shark finning, 49

University of California in Santa
  Barbara (UCSB), 26
University of Edinburgh
  (England), 14
U.S. Army, 42–43

Vancouver, George, 31–32
Voyage of the "Beagle," The
  (Darwin), 28

Westminster Abbey, 14
whales, 32–33
Wikelski, Martin
  on feral cats and dogs, 37
Wolf Volcano, 79
World Wildlife Fund, 35, 57

Picture Credits

About the Author

James Barter received his undergraduate degree in history and classics at the University of California (Berkeley) followed by graduate studies in ancient history and archaeology at the University of Pennsylvania. Mr. Barter has taught history as well as Latin and Greek.

A Fullbright scholar at the American Academy in Rome, Mr. Barter worked on archaeological sites in and around the city as well as on sites in the Naples area. He also has worked and traveled extensively in Greece.

Mr. Barter currently lives in Rancho Santa Fe, California, with his fifteen-year-old daughter Kalista who enjoys soccer, the piano, and mathematics. His older daughter, Tiffany Modell, also lives in Rancho Santa Fe and works as a violin teacher and music consultant.